"Small teams, big teams—all face big challenges. No one addresses those challenges more biblically, clearly, realistically, or helpfully than Stephen Macchia. If you're part of any ministry team, don't skip this book."

Larry Crabb, founder, New Way Ministries

"Of the many ways of being 'great,' team 'greatness' is one of the least explored and understood. Macchia's approach to building a great team is a major contribution to the literature."

Leonard Sweet, Drew University,
George Fox Evangelical Seminary, preachingplus.com

"My good friend Steve Macchia has hit another home run with *Becoming a Healthy Team*. Winning teams have discovered that intimacy with God must be the first priority. Steve has written a compelling and engaging book that will cause team leaders to rethink how they lead. Steve has led many successful organizations and teams in large-scale, fruitful events. He is widely respected by his team members and is one of the most well-read individuals I know on the important subject of effective leadership. This is a must read for leaders who aspire to build a biblical Spirit-led team."

Luis Palau, evangelist;
author, *High Definition Life*

"Stephen Macchia writes enthusiastically and cogently about the potential of 'teams' to bring new life to churches . . . teams in which participants share a common mission, honor Jesus Christ, accomplish meaningful ministry, and anticipate transformative results. Writing from many years of experience as a pastor, teacher, and church consultant, the author reminds readers that the top priorities of such teams are to experience intimacy with God and to build intimacy and authenticity in community with the family of God. If you would like to see the focus of church teams and committees shift from 'churchianity' to Christianity, this is an important book for you to read."

George H. Gallup Jr., founding chairman,
George H. Gallup International Institute

percent of the practical wisdom and God-honoring principles in *Becoming a Healthy Team*. I know Steve. I've observed him with his teams, and he's the real deal. This book is a keeper."

John Pearson, president and CEO,
Christian Management Association

"Don't read this book if you are looking for reasons to organize a church into teams or theoretical foundations for team ministry. This is one of the most practical books that will help everyone who is involved in a team ministry from team leaders right down to every person on the team. The book has a lot of practical material that works."

Elmer L. Towns, vice president, Liberty University; dean,
School of Religion, Lynchburg, Virginia

"In his new book, *Becoming a Healthy Team*, Dr. Steve Macchia addresses one of the most desperate needs facing the church today: how to become a healthy, highly functioning ministry team that God can use to advance his kingdom through the local church. Steve has learned these invaluable lessons through his many ministry successes leading people as teams. His practical advice and recommendations along each step of the way are a strong point of this book. If you want to build a strong, healthy, ministry team that God will work in and through, you'll want to read this book!"

Dr. Sam Rima, director, Bethel Seminary Doctor of Ministry
Program; author, *Leading from the Inside Out*

"Healthy leadership teams are the key to healthy ministries. Here is an excellent book that covers all the bases."

Dan Chun, senior pastor, First Presbyterian Church of Honolulu;
cofounder and president, Hawaiian Islands Ministries

"*Becoming a Healthy Team* collects some of the best resources available on effective teams and develops them into wisdom packages. Use Macchia's thoughtful book like a reference guide, and select the insight you need for your team's lasting benefit."

Dr. Bruce McNichol, coauthor, *The Ascent of a Leader* and
TrueFaced; president, Leadership Catalyst

"If you are serious about building a healthy team, then this is the book for you. Every chapter is pure gold and contains rich insights from team member selection to building and sustaining community. If you don't make this a part of your library—you have missed it."

Rodney L. Cooper, Kenneth and Jean Hansen
Professor of Discipleship and Leadership,
Gordon-Conwell Theological Seminary

"The buzz on healthy teams tells us that everyone wants one, but few know how to build one. To many leaders, attempts to form a healthy team resulted in hurt, anguish, and disappointment. To others they brought joy, excitement, and great accomplishment. Stephen Macchia communicates both the heart and skill of bringing together a healthy team. No one is better qualified to write this book. Anyone who cares about effective team ministry should read it."

Gary L. McIntosh, D.Min., Ph.D.,
Talbot School of Theology, Biola University

"Healthy teams need a strong conceptual framework and practical steps on which to grow and succeed. *Becoming a Healthy Team* will help your team to refine both its thinking and its action to lead your ministry to greater effectiveness."

Dave Travis, senior vice president, Leadership Network

"*Becoming a Healthy Team* is *the* manual for all who wish to serve and lead in effective ministry teams."

George K. Brushaber, president, Bethel University

"*Becoming a Healthy Team* provides powerful, biblical concepts capable of transforming your own leadership team. Macchia presents compelling truths about teams that can be understood and embraced by teams of all types in organizations of all sizes. The book provides valuable, original thought and also serves as an excellent resource for the best concepts articulated by other key authors in recent years. The ultimate benefit is a memorable framework to talk about and live out the dynamics of a healthy team—all to God's glory!"

Mark Johnson, executive vice president,
Evangelical Christian Credit Union

"Steve Macchia is an excellent leader of teams and comes from a long line of successful and learning-filled teams. His expertise in church leadership and ministry groups makes this book heavy with experiential wealth. This wealth of experience translates here into immanently practical insights about the reality of team. You will find here a wonderful balance of focus on team members *and* getting the task done with excellence. Begin this book exactly where you are . . . and end it further along the journey into healthy teams and team leadership."

Warren Schuh, executive pastor, Calvary Community Church,
Westlake Village, California

"*Becoming a Healthy Team* hits the nail on the head—again and again! Steve Macchia has an exceptional grasp of what it takes to build a winning team, than which nothing is more essential for a thriving, growing church. Steve not only understands team building, he has exemplified it in his own ministry. Read this excellent book by a master of the art and see what miracles can happen in and for the cause of Christ."

Donald W. Morgan, minister emeritus, First Church of Christ,
Wethersfield, Connecticut; author, *Share the Dream, Build the Team* and *When Your World Is Coming Apart*

"If we are going to fulfill God's Great Commission for his kingdom, then our teams must pay attention to God's collective call to service. Simple but compelling, Steve Macchia's book challenges us with a new breath of insight to reshape our teams for the vision Christ has given us."

Wayne Cordeiro, senior pastor, New Hope Christian Fellowship,
Honolulu, Hawaii

Becoming a Healthy Team

Five Traits of Vital Leadership

Stephen A. Macchia

BakerBooks
Grand Rapids, Michigan

© 2005 by Stephen A. Macchia

Published by Baker Books
a division of Baker Publishing Group
P.O. Box 6287, Grand Rapids, MI 49516-6287
www.bakerbooks.com

Printed in the United States of America

Library of Congress Cataloging-in-Publication Data
Macchia, Stephen A., 1956-
    Becoming a healthy team : five traits of vital leadership / Stephen A. Macchia.
        p.   cm.
    Includes bibliographical references.
    ISBN 0-8010-6572-0 (pbk.)
    1. Group ministry 2. Teams in the workplace. 3. Sports teams. 4. Christian leadership. 5. Leadership—Religious aspects—Christianity. I. Title.
BV675.M27 2005
253′.7—dc22   2005014387

This book is dedicated to the
Glory of God
Father, Son, and Holy Spirit
Blessed Trinity
Perfect in Power, Love, and Purity
True Head of Every Healthy Team

Contents

Acknowledgments

This book was a team effort from start to finish, not the writing of the manuscript but the development of the content. The principles of team health articulated in the following pages have grown out of nearly three decades of service to the body of Christ.

The first ministry team I led was an energetic group of committed believers who cared about the spiritual growth of junior high students at Grace Chapel in Lexington, Massachusetts. It is here where most of my transferable concepts were first formulated. After youth ministry, I was privileged to serve teams for more than a decade in children's ministry, adult ministry, and as senior associate pastor. To my Grace Chapel team colleagues in the 1970s and '80s, thank you for your investment in my life and ministry.

The fourteen years I spent at the helm of the Evangelistic Association of New England, later known as Vision New England, became the seedbed for team development at its finest. During my tenure, the team multiplied in size and complexity, eventually growing to 70 staff, 150 regional advisors, 13 board members, more than 1,000 members, and hundreds of volunteers, serving 6,000 congregations representing more than 80 denominations. Leading a team of this magnitude was exhilarating for me. To the entire Vision New England ministry family I offer profound gratitude.

With the new Leadership Transformations, Inc. (LTi) team, as well as my colleagues at Gordon-Conwell Theological Seminary, my team-building experience is combined with that of incredibly gifted leaders and is bearing fruit in new ways. Our shared labors of love are evidenced in the local church and parachurch leaders and teams that we equip for greater effectiveness as spiritual leaders. It's pure joy to watch ministries flourish as a result of our times together in spiritual formation–based leadership development experiences. To the board, staff, committees, and constituents represented in the LTi community, God bless you abundantly for allowing us the joy of coming alongside others "for such a time as this."

Too numerous to mention are my team of friends and extended family who have poured courage into my soul with generous love and prayers throughout my years of ministry. You have been my ongoing sustenance, conscience, advocates, prayer warriors, support team, and several (you know who!) my band of brothers. I'm not sure where I would be today had it not been for your rock-solid encouragement. I thank my God on every remembrance of you.

To the Baker Publishing Group team, I offer heartfelt thanks for believing in me several years ago when my publishing journey began. Your servant hearts are a wonder to behold. May the Lord richly bless the work of your hands.

Finally, and most important, my family team is second to none. Ruth, Nate, and Bekah are all star players who are faithful and true to the end, without whom I could never have survived the challenges that have accompanied the plentiful joys of team ministry. You are God's special gift to me, for whom I am eternally grateful.

Foreword

I first met Steve Macchia in 1977. We were both aspiring youth workers, zealous for service, and determined to make a difference for the kingdom of Christ. We've been friends ever since, and because of our long and deep friendship, I am thrilled and honored to be able to write this foreword to *Becoming a Healthy Team*.

Building on his previous books (*Becoming a Healthy Church* and *Becoming a Healthy Disciple*), Steve offers a well-researched delineation of what makes a team work. Drawing from his breadth of personal and ministry experience, Steve takes us into the Scriptures, especially the book of 1 Corinthians, and sheds new light on biblical teaching about community.

Becoming a Healthy Team is unique in the literature on teamwork because Steve takes great concepts and explains them in user-friendly terms, using illustrations with which every reader can identify. The T-E-A-M-S acrostic is a tool that you will find immediately usable, whether you're building a ministry team at your church, in your organization, at your workplace, or even within your own family. The big ideas—Trust, Empowerment, Assimilation, Managing, Service—will become measuring sticks for you and your team by which you can evaluate your progress. And the end-of-chapter discussion questions will enable your team to discuss the concepts and plan objectively for growth toward team health.

Becoming a Healthy Team is unique in the literature on teamwork because Steve is not afraid to address the difficult issues. Rather than just offering a host of motivational stories that are beyond most of our experiences, he reminds us that teamwork is work and that building a healthy team means growth—even through our failures together. Steve exhorts us to remember that teamwork is missional; without the service component, a team falls short of God's design. And Steve challenges us to see the concept of the body of Christ in a new light, reminding us that being united in our diversity and dependent on each other is Jesus' desire for our teams.

I believe in *Becoming a Healthy Team* because I believe in the unique guy who wrote it. We served on a church staff together for more than a decade. Now we're involved in separate ministries with other teams, but we still meet weekly for mutual encouragement and to give each other feedback and advice. I know the author well, and I know his extensive experience in and profound commitment to building healthy teams.

Don't read this book just because I believe in it. Read it because God will use its truths to transform the way you think about teamwork. I encourage you to read this book alone, to evaluate your personal team experiences (past and present). Read it with objective friends, to honestly assess where you and your team need strengthening. And then read it with your team, so that you can determine together how to work toward becoming healthier. *Becoming a Healthy Team* delivers what the title promises. The truths in this book will help your team achieve optimum health and maximum spiritual impact.

Paul Borthwick
Senior Consultant
Development Associates International

Introduction

The Truth about Teams

It's five o'clock in the morning. I'm two and a half years late in completing this manuscript for Baker Books. "Life" showed up and kept me from finding those necessary blocks of time for creative writing. In addition, I realize there are bigger reasons why it's taken me so long to finally get to the writing of this book. If I had done it any earlier, it would have looked too much like other people's writings on the subject. It would have had the feel of an extended research paper with footnotes, quotes, and anecdotes followed by application ideas that I had not tried but had learned from others. I guess that's why I'm bleary-eyed in front of the computer on the 17,437th day of my life, finally getting started on this long-anticipated project.

No, this book is not what I thought it would be three years ago when the publisher approved the idea. It's really quite different, mostly because I am a different person today, a transformed leader and a ministry team man with a changed heart about how to get the real work done. Most important, it's a distinct manuscript because I've had a series of "ah-ha experiences" over these intense few years, particularly in developing brand-new ministry offerings through Leadership Transformations (the group where I serve as team leader), as well as working with several teams as an outsider, coming alongside the leader to facilitate the shaping of team life from the inside out.

Teams are very difficult to create. They are tougher to motivate. They are impossible to predict. They can be challenging to lead. They can inspire greatness and they can embody pettiness. They can gel quickly and they can splinter apart overnight. They are filled with people who are unique in their backgrounds, hurts, needs, joys, desires, gifts, aspirations, and call. To get a diverse group of people working on the same page is the ongoing priority and challenge for leaders.

I know this from firsthand experience. For my entire ministry career I have been working with teams. I've led them and served on them, coached and prayed for them. I've built new teams and reengineered tired ones. I've seen teams flourish in unity and watched teams stagger and crumble in disunity. I know the joys and triumphs as well as the heartaches and failures of team ministry. Nothing I hear about teams today surprises me, for they are a challenge to build, a joy to equip, and a necessity if ministry is to thrive. It's time to wake up to this reality. We must do everything within our power to build teams that will accomplish beyond measure what God supernaturally intends.

My experience has not focused on athletic teams, since the extent of my athletic abilities is limited. I'm not a business team leader either, having lived my adult vocational life exclusively in local church and nonprofit parachurch ministry settings. But my experience is in working with people of all ages (children, youth, and adults) from many backgrounds (socioeconomic, political, religious, and ethnic) in a variety of settings (small, medium, and large churches, as well as small and medium-sized ministries), for an extensive number of purposes, and for nearly thirty years.

Not only have I grown to love working with teams but I am passionate about their importance. My passion has grown out of genuine love for people and an earnest desire to see them flourish in their life in Christ and in the context of their service to Christ and within the community of his church. My passion has come out of the pleasure and the pain of teams, both when I was fully engaged in building a team and on those days when I was ready to walk away out of hurt, anguish, and deep disappointment.

The Truth about Teams

It's time for leaders and ministries to consider the truth about team building. The crux of the matter is teams are a lot of work! This is because they are filled with sinful people who are in the process of becoming, or struggling against, all that God intends for them. There are several characteristics of teams that make them difficult to lead, characteristics such as their *composition* and *complexity*, which present a *challenge* to leadership. The required *commitment* of time can also be difficult. Teams are successful when they understand their *calling* and there is *continuity* in leadership, even though the team itself may *change*. Another challenge is the *conduct* of the team. All of this requires *courage* on the part of the team leader.

The *composition* of every team in ministry is unique, because the members of the team are unique. Therefore, it's incumbent on the leaders of every team to get to know the members of the team. Getting to know them requires that we spend time together, not only discussing the ministry we share but engaging in dialogue about the life we live.

Teams are unique not only in their composition but in their *complexity*. Because of the special makeup of each team, a leader discovers how complex the mixture becomes when all of these diverse people start to interrelate. Since we are not mechanical robots, we can't be programmed to act in a certain way during distinct moments. Quite the contrary. The challenge for leaders of teams is to be fully aware of the complexity and alert to the needs of each member as well as of the whole team all at the same time.

The composition and complexity of teams leads to the *challenge* of teams. To lead a team well is to be fully aware of the challenge and time commitment required to become a healthy team. Teams don't grow to maturity easily or quickly. We will cover the stages of development that teams experience later in this book, but for now let's own the realization that team leadership requires anticipation, forethought, creativity, and the agility to respond quickly to needs; all of this in addition to a *commitment* of time that is not fully recognized until well into one's season of service. We will return again and again to the challenge of building healthy teams.

What is the glue that holds teams together? It's the *calling* of teams to a particular missional purpose. Unless there is a focal point toward which their energies can be directed, a team is simply a meandering group of happy cohorts. There are far too many such groups in the church today. A group without a mission is like a shopper on a shopping spree who finds nothing to buy. Each member of the team needs to know with certainty the call of God on his or her life. The best gift the leader can offer is clarity of definition for the whole team and for each participant on the team. When the team members understand and focus on the mission, the team's calling can be fulfilled.

Since the team's calling is central to the purpose and priority for its existence, the leader's role is to provide a sense of *continuity* in fulfilling the mission and ministry amid the inevitable *changing* nature of teams. We often think of continuity when we consider those who are involved in teams, and that is a very important factor. But continuity of personnel lasts only so long before change occurs. The fact of the matter is any time a person joins or leaves the team, the whole team changes. So, if our primary goal is continuity of personnel, the mission may be compromised. The ministry must remain front and center. The needs of those being served must always outweigh those doing the serving. Therefore, we need to learn to accept the fluidity of coming and going that occurs on most teams, all the while working toward the long-term commitment of members and the vitality of ministry to others. The pruning that occurs when team members come and go may in fact be best for the ministry, though this truth about teams may be difficult for leaders to accept.

The *conduct* of teams promises to stretch the leader and requires *courage* to handle the people issues that will crop up almost on a daily basis. One never knows how team members may surprise the leader and one another by what they say or do. Maintaining a sense of equilibrium no matter the circumstances will help leaders and teams survive the ebb and flow of ministry life together. Courage on the leader's part requires a sense of the backdrop or reasons why people act and react the way they do. A wise leader will understand the story beneath the surface that may be driving a member to a certain behavior. It is important to remember that team members join a team asking basically the same series of questions:

- Why am I here?
- Why are you here?
- Whom are we serving and what are their needs?
- What shall we do together?
- How shall we do what we are called to do?
- When will we know that our task is complete?

As the *characteristics* of a team are explored, these questions are answered, and the answers reveal the health of the team. There are five essential traits of a healthy team, which I will describe in the following chapters. Put very simply, the traits are:

- Trust—Healthy teams trust.
- Empower—Healthy teams empower.
- Assimilate—Healthy teams assimilate.
- Manage—Healthy teams manage.
- Serve—Healthy teams serve.

The first letters of these traits form the acronym TEAMS. The traits are the backbone to ministry team health and vitality. They are required if a team is to experience the abundant life in the context of service. When a team leader desires to create an environment in which team members are fully engaged in the joy of team ministry, these traits are essential.

When intimacy and authenticity are part of team interactions, there is vitality. The five traits produce intimacy, authenticity, and vitality. *Intimacy* is embodied in *trust* and *empowerment*. *Authenticity* is enriched through *assimilation*. *Vitality* is evidenced in *management* and *service*.

Cooperation Not Competition

The Battle of Britain which lasted from August 8th to October 31st, 1940 cost the Germans 2,375 planes destroyed in daylight alone, and many more at night. It cost the British 375 pilots killed and 358 wounded. A handful of RAF fliers had saved Britain, and perhaps the world, from destruction. Do you remember how Winston Churchill spoke for his people: "Never in the field of human conflict was so much owed by so many to so few!" That victory was achieved you see, not by the top-ranking generals, the brass hats, the big shots, but by young men—a team—playing and fighting . . . and dying together.[1]

Winning battles is a wartime motif that many have utilized in defining teams, and for good reason. In wartime it's important to know who the enemy is and what resources you have available to beat the enemy. But far too often we take this analogy into the life of the church. We forget that there is only one enemy that every single Christian ministry team is fighting against—the enemy of our souls. The enemy is not each other. The enemy is not another church down the street or a different denomination or a similar ministry or even a member of our own church. No, the enemy is Satan, the destroyer of teams and the archenemy of every healthy ministry endeavor.

The only acceptable competition on a team is against that one enemy. In Christian community the only acceptable option among teams and team members is *cooperation*. Our primary mission is to cooperate with one another in shared endeavors to beat the one and only enemy that seeks to devour the cooperative spirit of God's people.

Unfortunately, we've succumbed to competitive thinking in today's ministry settings. We've got it all wrong. The Bible doesn't set us up to fight against each other! Therefore, whenever we use analogies that lead to that conclusion, we are missing the point. For example, when we use athletic illustrations to justify our competitive edge in ministry, we are creating a competitive, one-upmanship, us-versus-them mentality—and it's rarely against the "enemy"; it's against each other. When we use corporate analogies for team building, we refer to ministry with bottom-line, financial implications, always seeking ways to put a positive spin on difficult times and ultimately creating climates of competition where we are unwilling to speak the full truth in authentic love. When we use socioeconomic illustrations for teams, we focus more on geography and material gain and ethnic divisions than on finding ways to share the abundance of resources in a unifying way with those who are different from us. When we use political ideologies in establishing teams, we lean toward power plays, manipulation, and selfish gain. Even though we can learn a lot about how to function as a team from these worldly examples of team life and development, we must remember that competition should not be the driving force behind our efforts.

Pick up a copy of your favorite Christian magazine. What do the ads connote to you? Are the colleges, publishers, conferences, seminaries, service groups, and any other advertisers listed there in competition with others who are also paying for prime advertising space in the same periodical? When you go to a Christian conference, are the vendors there to help you choose the best option for your life or ministry, or are they trying to convince you to select only their product? When you consider the needs of your local church ministry, do you find competitive tactics employed to lure you in only one direction of service, or is your church one that helps each individual find the best place for him or her to utilize gifts, resources, time, and energy?

The Christian worldview must inform our understanding of Christian ministry teams. Christian teams know that they are to work cooperatively not competitively. They know that there is strength in diversity and multi-ethnicity not in separation and division in the body. They know that Christ's priority mission is the church, and it's not to be unduly influenced by the world of corporate schemes that include manipulation of data or people's lives. Christian leaders and teams understand that heart matters more than head knowledge or skills, for if the heart is right with God, the head and hands will follow.

It's time we turn our understanding of healthy teams right side up! The godly team of the twenty-first century cares deeply about the claims of Christ being fulfilled in their ministry environment and in the context of their specific team. The Christ-honoring team embraces the challenge of living in community together and seeking ways to complement and empower others to be the best that God called them to be. A healthy team freely, lovingly, and generously cheers others on to victory against the real enemy of our souls, not against other Christians, churches, ministries, or endeavors that are also seeking to build up the kingdom of God.

When the heart of the leader and every member of the team is pursuing intimacy with Christ as a personal and daily priority, then cooperation will be a natural by-product of life together in ministry. Intimacy with Christ and the corresponding overflow of love will guide the team into a deeper place of service that will reap eternal fruit and life-transforming ministry, lasting longer than any one of the lives currently on the team. Let's get it right once and for all—healthy teams are God's design, and the result of building such teams is a slice of heaven on earth.

Your Primary Mission

All teams have a title—staff team, ministry team, elder team, missions team, youth team, outreach team, administrative team, and so on. Each member of the team has a title—chairperson, director, teacher, small group leader, administrator, pastor, and so on. Our titles define our mission and we focus our attention on fulfilling it as well as possible throughout our years of service together.

But in reality our central mission is not expressed by our title. What we do together is not our most important mission. That mission, defined by its label, is our secondary mission.

Our priority mission is intimacy with God, and our secondary mission is intimacy and authenticity in community with the family of God. Our outcome mission is vitality in well-managed service to others. If and when we finally figure this out, we will indeed be on the road to becoming a healthy team.

Therefore, an approach to team development that is distinctly cooperative, unapologetically Christ-centered, and explicitly designed to deepen the soul of leaders and team members is where we are heading in our treatment of team life. When each team member keeps intimacy with God in the forefront, the end result will be a spiritually healthy team. This is to be our explicit goal and our top priority.

The spiritual vitality of the team evidences itself in deep relationships with one another and effective service to others. There is no other way. For many years in the midst of a hectic schedule and high demands on my time and energy, I forgot this truth. I found myself leading on the run, and the team followed suit. It wasn't until I hit a wall and discovered I was at the end of my resources that I finally found help in returning to where I needed to be—in the place where my walk with God is the most important responsibility in my job description, enabling me to lead and participate in ministry teams with spiritual energy and commitment. It is there where my life begins and ends, and everything in between is affected by the quality (or lack thereof) of the spiritual life I choose. As I experience the abundant life in Christ and encourage this in others, together we can conquer the corner of the universe that is ours to serve, all in the name of Jesus.

Do you feel trapped as a leader and a team member by the demands on your time and energy? Are you busy doing the work of God and missing out on the joyful vitality of a walk with God? Then you are an established member of the activity-driven, mo-tivated-by-the-demands-of-others, filled-yet-unfulfilled world of today's average team member.

You don't have to reside in that state of heart and mind any longer. There is a more excellent way. It's the way of love, found in the depth of your soul, the richness of his Word, the delight of prayer, and the welcoming invitation to come close that the

Lord Jesus issues to you daily. Take him up on his offer, hop up in his lap, lean totally in his direction, find comfort for your soul, listen for his still small voice, and delight in doing his will. Once you experience the richness of this fellowship, your life will overflow in service to all who cross your path.

A Team Member's Prayer

Loving Father, blessed Son, Holy Spirit, I want to live in the abundance of your joy this day. As I serve you on the team to which you have called me, I embrace the challenge of mutual ministry with friends and colleagues who are diverse and distinct. Grant to me your faithful heart that longs for intimacy with me and give me the courage to be authentic with my brothers and sisters in Christ with whom I share ministry. May the words of my mouth and the meditations of my heart be acceptable in your sight, O Lord, my Rock and my Redeemer. In the name of your Son, Jesus. Amen.

For Reflection

1. What is the truth about your team (its composition, complexity, and challenges)? What energizes you about your team and what most concerns you about your team?
2. What is the level of intimacy and authenticity in relationship with God and one another on your team? How will the depth of intimacy and authenticity impact the vitality of your shared service in the days ahead?
3. What is your response to the basic premise of this book—that we are to build ministry teams that foster community and cooperation (instead of embracing a corporate mindset that leads to competition among members and with other churches, ministries, or teams)?
4. In what ways can your team address the issues of deepening commitment to one another as you begin to sort through issues of team health and vitality?
5. What excites you the most about the prospect of becoming a healthy team?

1

The Bible and Teams

When First Parish finally sought assistance, the church was in trouble. Attendance was dropping fast. The leaders were more concerned about who was leaving than who was staying. Old ways of doing church were no longer working and families with young children and the youth were virtually absent. Special music had been dropped from the liturgy because it had become too much of an ego trip for the soloists. The organist was older than the pipe organ but unwilling to give up her bench. The church building was falling apart, and the neighborhood was unhappy with the property's decline. Outreach was nonexistent, and relationships were faltering everywhere.

When First Parish reached out for help, the person they hired started talking about the quality of their life, worship, and witness. The vision, mission, and ministries of First Parish needed review. The consultant challenged the church to consider a team approach to leadership that would begin addressing the most pressing issues, and he urged the pastor to share some of the load, inviting others from the congregation to help.

After the first meeting with this outside helper, the pastor immediately called the denominational headquarters. Something about teams was really bothering this leader. So he said to the superintendent, "The word *team*—I don't find it in any of my concordances. Is it in the Bible and does God really sanction such an idea?" The superintendent agreed that the team concept was not biblical and discouraged him from following the consultant's advice. Two years later the church is ready to close its doors. No team remains.

The denominational leader was right on one count. The word *team* doesn't appear in the English Bible. Otherwise he was dead wrong. The team idea is everywhere in the Bible. It appears in places where God describes his children as the people of God and the family of God. He even goes so far as to call his earthly family a chosen people, a royal priesthood, a holy nation, a people belonging to God (1 Peter 2:9). All of these descriptions suggest our modern-day understanding of team.

George Barna reminds us:

> God's Word does not make a big deal about the importance of leaders serving in teams. Most of the wisdom gleaned regarding teams must be drawn from passages or stories in which the key principles relate to other aspects of life and ministry. In fact, while I believe the Bible is a great text on leadership, it directly discusses leadership in relatively few passages; most leadership principles derived from the Bible are inferential.[1]

Even so, with the Bible as our source for understanding teams, there are many places to reference that provide more than enough justification for First Parish (and every other church and parachurch ministry) to pursue a team-based approach to ministry.

God's Truth about Teams

Scattered throughout the Scriptures, God's people provide great examples of partnerships and teams. Often in the Bible the Lord makes clear that he delights to see his children functioning in unity. Without a doubt, God supports the significance and priority of teams. Here are some examples of God's teams:

- The Trinity. Father, Son, and Holy Spirit are the perfect team, working together from time past throughout all eternity!
- Adam and Eve (Genesis 2–3). From the creation garden where conception and subsequent procreation began, two became one flesh, which ultimately multiplied life for every subsequent generation.
- Noah and his family (Genesis 6–9). Overcoming all odds to build an ark for God, Noah accomplished the monumental task that brought about a rainbow of promises outlining God's care for all of his creation.
- Jacob's son Joseph and his jealous brothers (Genesis 37, 45, 49, 50). Brothers serving on the same family team should have been so right, but it all went sour for several years. Eventually Joseph redeemed the team when he said to his brothers: "'Don't be afraid. Am I in the place of God? You intended to harm me, but God intended it for good to accomplish what is now being done, the saving of many lives. So then, don't be afraid. I will provide for you and your children.' And he reassured them and spoke kindly to them" (50:19–21).
- Moses and Jethro, his father-in-law (Exodus 18). Seeing the way in which Moses was leading, Jethro suggested that Moses divide up the leadership responsibilities and start delegating duties with others who were gifted and capable. Listening to his father-in-law, Moses did everything he said and "chose capable men from all Israel and made them leaders of the people, officials over thousands, hundreds, fifties and tens" (v. 25). Moses' team served well together and saved Moses the burden of carrying the load of leadership all on his own.
- Aaron, Hur, and Moses. Just prior to Moses' encounter with Jethro, we see Aaron and Hur coming alongside Moses to lift his hands and support him in his prayers

(Exod. 17:12–13). "When Moses' hands grew tired, they took a stone and put it under him and he sat on it. Aaron and Hur held his hands up—one on one side, one on the other—so that his hands remained steady till sunset" (v. 12). Teamwork prevails even in times of prayer!

- Joshua, following in the footsteps of Moses (Joshua 23). After living a full life as a faithful leader, Joshua summoned all Israel—elders, leaders, judges, and officials—and said, "Be very strong; be careful to obey all that is written in the Book of the Law of Moses, without turning aside to the right or to the left. . . . You are to hold fast to the LORD your God, as you have until now" (vv. 6, 8). The team surrounding Joshua would carry on his legacy and fulfill their shared destiny.

- Nehemiah and his fellow workers. On a campaign to restore the city walls, Nehemiah leaned fully on the skills of others on the team to accomplish this larger-than-life goal (Nehemiah 2–7). Nehemiah was "carrying on a great project" (6:3) and fulfilled the call of God on his life through faithful service as a leader of a team of men whom God listed by name (see Nehemiah 3).

- Job and his wife and friends. Tested to the brink, with losses unthinkable and pain that most would consider intolerable, Job was teamed up with his wife and three friends who helped him interpret his woes. This example of teamwork reminds us that even those who appear to be godly assistants can indeed misinterpret the will and work of God and encourage us to give up and even despair. Teams of this ilk are more plentiful than not, and they all began in places like the land of Uz!

- Shadrach, Meshach, and Abednego (Daniel 3). These three emerged from the fiery furnace as servants of the Most High God without a single hair of their heads singed, no strand of their robes scorched, and no smell of fire on them (vv. 26–27). As a result of the faithfulness of this team, who defied the king's command and were willing to give up their lives rather than serve or worship any god except their own God, Nebuchadnezzar praised God.

- Jesus and his disciples (Matthew 10 and numerous other Gospel passages). Jesus sent the Twelve out to fulfill his mission, share his message, and perform life-changing ministry. This motley group of called-out ones was privileged to partner with the Savior in ministry beyond measure. The likes of the disciples are known today as followers of Christ who are willing to die to self so that the life, love, and mission of Christ may be evidenced in this world.
- The early church (most of the book of Acts). From the time of Pentecost to the earliest growth of the Christian church, the believers were known to share all they had with one another so that the mission, message, and ministry of Christ would be multiplied in their generation. The ripple effects of this movement of the Spirit remain actively alive today—hallelujah!
- The apostle Paul and other missionaries (Acts 9, 13, and other accounts of Paul's missionary journeys). Known for his strident accusations and condemnations of Christians, the apostle Paul experienced a dramatic conversion. After that he teamed up at various times with Silas, Barnabas, John Mark, and Timothy, traveling from city to city establishing churches throughout Asia Minor. His work could not have been successful had it not been for the teams he rallied, trained, challenged, and supported in their development during the earliest years of Christianity.

These are just some of the examples of teamwork God has preserved for our study and reflection as we consider the needs and traits of healthy teams today. A few others you may wish to examine include the partnerships of Ruth and Naomi, Esther and Mordecai, David and Jonathan, Saul and his armies. The point here is that God cares deeply about fulfilling his love and lordship through teams of men and women who share a common heart for God and an earnest desire to accomplish much more together than they could ever do alone.

Imagine if the pastor of First Parish and the denominational executive thumbed their way through the Scriptures to discover whether teams are valid. Would they have stumbled on these and other examples of God-empowered teamwork?

United as One Body

In addition to the multiple examples of biblical teams noted above, my all-time favorite illustration of a team is found in a powerful image of the people of God. This illustration is in 1 Corinthians 12, where the apostle Paul provides an excellent description of the body of Christ—the ultimate team. Here is the text in which I have changed the word *body* to *team* for emphasis. I also point out how the traits of T-E-A-M-S—trusting, empowering, assimilating, managing, and serving—can be seen in the body.

> T—The *team* is a unit, though it is made up of many parts; and though all its parts are many, they form one *team*. So it is with Christ (v. 12).

> E—For we were all baptized by one Spirit into one *team*— whether Jews or Greeks, slave or free—and we were all given the one Spirit to drink (v. 13).

> A—Now the *team* is not made up of one part but of many. If the foot should say, "Because I am not a hand, I do not belong to the *team*," it would not for that reason cease to be part of the *team*. And if the ear should say, "Because I am not an eye, I do not belong to the *team*," it would not for that reason cease to be part of the *team* (vv. 14–16).

> M—If the whole *team* were an eye, where would the sense of hearing be? If the whole *team* were an ear, where would the sense of smell be? But in fact God has arranged the parts of the *team*, every one of them, just as he wanted them to be. If they were all one part, where would the *team* be? (vv. 17–19).

> S—As it is, there are many parts, but one *team*.
> The eye cannot say to the hand, "I don't need you!" And the head cannot say to the feet, "I don't need you!" On the contrary,

those parts of the *team* that seem to be weaker are indispensable, and the parts that we think are less honorable we treat with special honor. And the parts that are unpresentable are treated with special modesty, while our presentable parts need no special treatment (vv. 20–24).

T—But God has combined the members of the *team* and has given greater honor to the parts that lacked it, so that there should be no division in the *team* (vv. 24–25),

E—but that its parts should have equal concern for each other (v. 25).

A—If one part suffers, every part suffers with it; if one part is honored, every part rejoices with it (v. 26).

M—Now you are the *team* of Christ, and each one of you is a part of it (v. 27).

S—And in the church God has appointed first of all apostles, second prophets, third teachers, then workers of miracles, also those having gifts of healing, those able to help others, those with gifts of administration, and those speaking in different kinds of tongues. Are all apostles? Are all prophets? Are all teachers? Do all work miracles? Do all have gifts of healing? Do all speak in tongues? Do all interpret? But eagerly desire the greater gifts.
And now I will show you the most excellent way (vv. 28–31).

Paul's use of the body to describe the people of God, working at their optimum level of effectiveness, is by far one of the greatest examples of team unity in the Scriptures. God's clear intention is for the church to be united. We see this throughout the Gospels, articulated with poignancy in Jesus' great prayer in John 17. It is magnified throughout the early church, as described for us in the book of Acts, exemplified in the writings of Paul, Peter, and John throughout the Epistles, and clarified once more in the book of Revelation where the church is called to faithfully adhere to Christ's priorities for all eternity.

The body of Christ is indeed a team, interwoven with perfection, just as God ordained from the dawn of creation. The parts of the body need each other to be a living organism. That's the church—not an organization but an organism, alive in the Spirit, serving side by side, enhancing one another's role, giving of one's self so that the other can thrive. The body analogy is the best one for teams because it describes the traits of healthy teams to a T.

Let's look again at how the traits of a healthy team can be seen in the 1 Corinthians 12 passage:

T—The team is one unit, the place where *trust* is born (v. 12).

E—One team, no matter our background, is *empowered* as individuals (v. 13).

A—Each part is *assimilated* with another, needing each other to belong (vv. 14–16).

M—The team is *managed* and arranged as God desires (vv. 17–19).

S—Team members *serve* no matter how weak, honorable, or presentable they are (vv. 20–24).

● ● ●

T—Because there is no division in a healthy team, there is *trust* (v. 25).

E—The team is *empowered* because each part has equal concern for the others (v. 25).

A—When *assimilated* empathetically, the team experiences suffering and rejoicing (v. 26).

M— The gifts of the Spirit are *managed* and distributed with care (v. 27).

S—Each gift of the team *serves* the greater priority of love (vv. 28–31).

Using 1 Corinthians 12 as our lens for understanding teamwork will deepen our commitment to the body of Christ. When we come to grips with the fact that the health of our ministry team is affected by our role within the body of Christ, we will be far better equipped to serve the church with zeal and vitality. This lens is the one we will use throughout our treatment of team development. With the body analogy as our backdrop, we will return regularly to our prayerful priority of becoming a healthy disciple who cares deeply about the quality of health within our team.

The Most Excellent Way

The most excellent way for teams to function is to *love*. The thirteenth chapter of 1 Corinthians magnifies the way the body of Christ (described in chapter 12) is to live. In this chapter the apostle Paul writes very specifically about the excellent way of love.

He begins the chapter focusing on what lovelessness looks like. He describes it as a resounding gong or a clanging cymbal, a "nothing," a zero on a scale of 1 to 10 (vv. 1–3). In other words, he is saying, don't speak of love, live it. Don't use your gifts without love, or you'll see nothing in return. Don't give all that you have to the poor without love, or what you give away will be empty and shallow. You gain nothing.

Instead, the call of God is to love in a selfless way. Verses 4–8 contrast what love is and what love is not.

What Love Is	What Love Is Not
patient	envious
kind	boastful
rejoices with the truth	proud
always protects	rude
always trusts	self-seeking
always hopes	easily angered
always perseveres	keeping a record of wrong
forever (never fails)	delighting in evil

For the health of the body—the eternal team of Christ—love is the answer to every question, the motivation for every decision, the reason for every relationship, and the result of every ministry. Love is the key to our health within the body and within every team. When love resides at the center of the team, God is there as well.

If you are looking for the most excellent way, then for God's sake, love.

A Team Prayer

Father, why is it that whenever we find ourselves faltering as a team, we look in every direction but yours? Forgive us for not responding to your loving initiatives on our behalf. Our team longs to do your will and to do so in such a way that we grow in our love for you. In the working out of our faith in the context of love, help us to trust you, empower one another, assimilate and complement the gifts and strengths that each brings to the team, manage with excellence, and serve with ever increasing joy.

To you and you alone belong all praise, honor, and glory. You are the Lord of the church, the Head of the body, the Cornerstone of our faith, the Reason we exist, the Leader of our team. Raise us up to love as Jesus loved, with a sacrificial heart and a longing to be in your presence every moment of the day. Thank you that teams matter so much to you and thank you for the privilege of joining hearts and hands and voices with others in the body of Christ that you have sent our way during this season of our life. We commit our team to you with great love and gratitude. In the strong name of our team leader, Jesus, we pray. Amen.

For Reflection

1. What are the primary ways you've discovered God's big ideas about teams? What stories in the Scriptures are most endearing to you that reinforce your understanding of God's view of teams?
2. If God were writing a story about your ministry team today, what would be the main plot lines that give definition to your experiences? Who are the main characters?

What most encourages you about the story being written in your shared ministry experiences?

3. Read through chapters 12 and 13 of 1 Corinthians. What is the apostle Paul saying to you and your team in these chapters? Begin to write out admonitions about developing team health from the pages of his Word and pray that these truths will become evident in your team.

4. Write your own prayer for your team, listing each member by name and asking God to unite you around his purposes and priorities for your ministry together in the coming months.

5. Discuss among your team various ways you can practice the most excellent way of love toward one another and those you serve.

2

Overview of Healthy Teams

When the Second Parachurch Ministry board of directors gathered around the table for their meetings, it was virtually impossible to impress on them that they needed to leave behind their own self-interests and pet projects. For whatever reason, the vice chairperson always had a story to share about her favorite charity in another city. The treasurer talked about his latest cruise with a group of Christian musicians and speakers. The newest member of the board had his sights set on starting a Christian school adjacent to his local church. The development chair was keenly interested in how his business supported other worthy causes. And the nominating committee chair was always promoting the way her husband ran their local ministry board.

Ever attend such a "team" meeting? If you've been in charge of a team and had people come to one of your meetings with other interests, agendas, or topics that drew people away from or even were in opposition to your focus, you know how frustrating this can be!

Teams that don't come together around a central mission, message, and ministry are merely wasting their time, and in many cases dismantling what others have built in the past.

When team members come to their task, they must focus on it single-mindedly. If their interests are diverted elsewhere, their attempts to work together can become a fiasco. It's essential that every team member concentrate on the task at hand and come to the table with his or her own self-interests left behind.

The Greatest Show on Earth

Craig This is a research associate at the Office of Research of the United Methodist Church. He was quoted by Dave Travis in a "Church Champions Update" concerning how much he had learned about teams at the circus![1] He outlines very clearly why it's important for team members to focus on the task at hand and not be encumbered by self-interests. At the circus Craig discovered afresh why members of a team need to consider the needs of their team members and the mission of the team as center-ring priority. He writes:

> Recently, my wife and I took our two sons, ages 6 and 2, to the Ringling Brothers Barnum and Bailey Circus. Watching the various acts and performances led me to draw some interesting conclusions about church work for church champions.
> It's all about teams and teamwork: Every act, every performance, and every job was performed in teams. From the threesome whose job it was to remove animal refuse (one sweeps and two shovel) to the high wire acts (one walks while the other hands the balancing pole), teams were prevalent everywhere. By using teams, the circus performers could quickly, efficiently, and safely handle a task, which meant little or no delays throughout the performance. This, in turn, kept the performance moving along as expected and kept the audience's attention on the performance and its message.
> The ringmaster isn't always the center of attention. For the most part, the ringmaster was heard, not seen, throughout the two and a half hour performance. The ringmaster's job was to direct the audience's attention and provide an introduction of the acts and performances for the audience. The ringmaster would set the context for each act, and, if necessary, provide

interpretation. He kept his and the audience's focus on the performance and its message.

If you fall, get up and try again: the breathtaking trapeze artists fly through the air, doing somersaults, twists, and flips. They catch one another and then throw one another. Every now and then, they would miss a catch or flip. The errant artist would fall into the net, bounce a few times, get up, climb the ladder back up to the trapeze, and in a matter of moments try again. Yes, it is a cliché, but the show must go on, and consequently, the performers would recover, quickly forget the mistake, and continue. As always, keeping the audience focused on the performance and the message.

I was amazed at the preparation, in terms of back-up materials for everything, so that "the show must go on." If a juggler riding on horseback dropped a ring or pin he or she was juggling, immediately a new set of pins or rings were handed up to that person. When a support post for a temporary net snapped, a second was quickly secured and put in place. No time was lost in getting the show back and the audience had little time to focus on the problem. Again, everything was centered on the performance and the message.

In the end, it comes down to the fact that Ringling Brothers Barnum and Bailey Circus knows that their mission is to "be the greatest show on earth." To that extent, they work very hard to ensure that everything they do works to achieve that mission and nothing, even the slightest mistake, distracts from that mission.

Christian ministry teams today have a lot to learn about maintaining focus on a commonly shared mission, message, and ministry. Far too often we are distracted from the central mission and find ourselves going off course and falling away from our priority message. As a result, we develop programs for the sake of activity rather than to accomplish ministry of fabulous proportions for God.

Often, though we call ourselves a team, we are simply a work group. We have banded together to offer our services to a ministry, but we are really there for our own self-interests. Work groups focus their attention on accomplishing goals through individuals who work on their own, whereas a team seeks to accomplish tasks interdependently. These are two distinct ways that people work together, both worthy of consideration, but when teamwork is the desired outcome, it's essential that we understand the difference between the two.

Jon Katzenbach and Douglas Smith, in their bestseller *The Wisdom of Teams*, suggest the following distinctions between a work group and a team.[2]

Work Group	Team
Strong, clearly focused leader	Shared leadership roles
Individual accountability	Individual and mutual accountability
Purpose is same as broader organization	Team purpose that the team delivers
Individual work-products	Collective work-products
Runs efficient meetings	Encourages open-ended discussions and active problem-solving meetings

A team functions as a whole, and although it needs and requires strong leadership, it doesn't revolve solely around one person. A healthy team works collectively, cooperatively, and complementarily, with each member contributing to the strength and vitality of the whole. When a team gathers for meetings and ministry, it is essential that members come with the full interests of the team in heart and mind. Otherwise, they may fall from the high wire, which can be devastating.

Be alert to this reality and watch the dynamics around the table at your next meeting. Are team members leaving behind the concerns of their own personal lives and other service opportunities to focus on your shared mission, message, and ministry? Then and only then will your collective efforts become your greatest gift for God on earth.

What Is a Team?

We have looked at the metaphor of the body (or even a well-run circus!) to describe the makeup of a team. Now we need to develop a workable definition of a Christ-centered team:

A Christian ministry team is a manageable group of diversely gifted people who hold one another accountable to serve joyfully together for the glory of God by:

- sharing a common mission
- embodying the loving message of Christ
- accomplishing a meaningful ministry
- anticipating transformative results

The key components of this definition are:

1. *A Christian ministry team.* This definition is descriptive of a distinctly Christian team, composed of those who serve together within a local church or parachurch ministry setting with Christ at the center of their endeavors.
2. *A manageable group.* A healthy team has a manageable number of members and is led by one team leader, functioning within a larger context of ministry.
3. *Diversely gifted people.* Each member of the team brings his or her unique set of gifts and abilities to complement others on the team.
4. *Hold one another accountable.* Mutual accountability is the goal in relationships within the team for the sake of synergy and ongoing effectiveness of the whole ministry.
5. *Joyfully serving together.* An attitude of joyfulness is the hallmark of quality servanthood and affects the life of the entire team experience.
6. *For the glory of God.* In a Christian context, everything the team does is to be for the glory of God and the expansion of his kingdom.
7. *Sharing a common mission.* Members come into the relationship with an earnest desire to move forward the mission and vision of the ministry team.
8. *Embodying the loving message of Christ.* How the team functions together is exhibited in their generous love for one another.

9. *Accomplishing a meaningful ministry.* The work of the team fulfills a goal worthy of their investment of time, talent, and treasure.
10. *Anticipating transformative results.* The team expects that God will multiply their shared labors of love on his behalf by exhibiting life-transformation in the hearts and lives of all whom the team serves.

This definition is fully consistent with our understanding from 1 Corinthians 12 of a healthy Christian team. We discover from the apostle Paul's writing that God designed the parts of the body to work interdependently in ways that honor God's purposes and priorities. When a team embraces this reality and pursues the richness of this kind of relationship and life together, the joys of service are exponentially achieved. However, among teams this is more often the exception than the rule.

Pastor and author George Cladis outlines how a vibrant twenty-first-century church ministry team reflects the fellowship and love of God. He summarizes the team characteristics that God uses to form and shape us into the people we are intended to be. The ministry team is covenanting, visionary, culture creating, collaborative, trusting, empowering, and learning.

> The ministry team that covenants together, articulates the church's vision, and creates a church culture that models collaboration and trust is also a team that is deepening its own sense of discipleship and learning. Ministry teams must be growing, learning teams. They are growing communities that are being shaped by the Spirit more and more in the image of God. These same teams experiment and take risks with what they have learned and experienced. Ministry teams are innovative, constantly seeking to apply their learning in practical ways. Their learning, both spiritual and practical, becomes a narrative of growth that can help other teams and churches grow spiritually and become more effective communities of ministry.[3]

Cladis is suggesting here that there are ways in which ministry teams can become high-performing Christian teams. Church and parachurch ministry settings that desire such attributes in their teams will discover that there is a pathway that leads to this maturity level. Becoming a spiritually healthy, highly effective ministry team takes time and effort. It requires the commitment of all team members, and each one must embrace a commonly understood definition of team and the characteristics of a healthy team.

Maturity of Teams

Like every human body, the spiritual body of Christ grows and matures in keeping with God's design. Every Christian ministry team is unique and matures in distinct ways, but the stages in the maturing process parallel the growth of a person through the stages of life:

- In our infancy, family is central to our well-being. Mother has given us life, father provides leadership, and siblings teach us that our world is bigger than ourselves.
- In our childhood, neighborhood is introduced. Family remains our place of stability from which we launch into friendships designed for learning and play.
- In our pre-adolescence, we first experience teams. From t-ball to Pop Warner football to pee-wee hockey, we begin to broaden our interests into the extended community and begin to lean on others for our shared success.
- In our adolescence, we learn about competition. Often, to our detriment and in a clumsy way, we discover that others share this planet with us. Our me-centeredness is challenged by the more pressing needs of others.
- In our adulthood, we move from varsity to alumni to starting our own family. We fall in love, find a vocation, become a professional, and begin the circle of life all over again.

- In our maturity, we coach and assist others, mentoring and helping them to thrive. The wisdom of our experience bears fruit in the hearts and lives of the next generation.

Teams grow in similar ways. For some ministry teams, it's all about "family." We stay in the infancy stage and learn to get along with others who are safe to be with and work alongside. We know each other well and are affectionate. We are generous and forgiving. But we don't go much beyond the four walls of our comfortable environment or venture out too far from home. This stage of team life is comfortable, compatible, and collegial.

As the ministry team matures, we venture out into the "neighborhood" and begin to reach out to others on the team who are different from us. We discover that others were raised in ways that are very foreign to our own life experience. We learn to accept one another's distinctives without having to confront our own uniqueness. The childhood stage of team development is still very playful and engaging. Even as members learn from and cooperate with one another, it's still a very safe stage.

When the ministry team hits adolescence, things can get very rocky and uncertain. At this point teams begin to see one another's dark side, and competition begins to emerge. If we hang in there long enough, however, and if we can avoid adolescent rebellion, the team will survive this stage. But the heartaches and headaches attached to adolescence emerge in ministry teams as much as in teenage life. When a team reaches this stage and immature behaviors arise, offending team members need to be confronted in love. In the adolescent stage of team development, the need for prayer and dependence on God emerges like never before. This is the stage that can either draw a team together or break it apart.

In the adulthood stage of team development, many of the parts and pieces of ministry are coming together. During this phase, the team experiences growth, stability, and advancement. In a team's adulthood, there is discussion about passing the ministry along to the next generation. In addition, the team becomes aware that they need to put structure, funding, and systems in place to last beyond their years. All of this leads into the next stage of team development—the season of maturity.

The goal is to get the team to its fullest form of expression and that's when it enters vibrant maturity. Here the team begins to see with much greater clarity the roles and responsibilities of each member in light of the bigger mission. In maturity the fully formed team functions out of love for one another and with mutual admiration and accountability. The team delights to see each member succeed in building up the entire body. When the team is fully functioning, then fruit blossoms forth in fulfillment of its shared mission and is multiplied in the hearts and lives of others. When mature teams bear fruit by creating a new generation of teams, the cycle of health is replicated and renewed.

Katzenbach and Smith describe the maturing process of teams with their team performance curve:

1. *Working group*. This is a group for which there is no significant incremental performance need or opportunity that would require it to become a team. The members interact primarily to share information, best practices, or perspectives and to make decisions to help each individual perform within his or her area of responsibility.

2. *Pseudo-team*. This is a group for which there could be a significant, incremental performance need or opportunity, but it has not focused on collective performance and is not really trying to achieve it. It has no interest in shaping a common purpose or set of performance goals, even though it may call itself a team. Pseudo-teams are the weakest of all groups in terms of performance impact.

3. *Potential team*. This is a group for which there is significant, incremental performance need, and that really is trying to improve its performance impact. Typically, however, it requires more clarity about purpose, goals, or work-products and more discipline in hammering out a common working approach.

4. *Real team*. This is a small number of people with complementary skills who are equally committed to a common purpose,

goals, and working approach for which they hold themselves mutually accountable.

5. *High-performance team.* This is a group that meets all the conditions of real teams, and has members who are also deeply committed to one another's personal growth and success. That commitment usually transcends the team. The high-performance team significantly outperforms all other like teams.[4]

Growing from a working group into a high-performance team takes time and patience on the part of team leaders and members. But the maturing process is workable for all teams, no matter the shape, size, purpose, or complexity. Becoming a healthy team is the process that leads teams to greater maturity and effectiveness.

Stages of Team Development

Students of team development recognize that teams go through various stages of development. One of the most popular characterizations is known as forming, norming, storming, and performing.[5] At each stage, the team leader has a different role to play.

Forming

When a team first comes together, everyone is trying to figure out how he or she will fit with each other. What are the team's goals? How do roles, tasks, and responsibilities play out? How much authority does one have to make decisions?

When I first arrived at Vision New England in the spring of 1989, the team was formed around our central priority of evangelism. We got to know one another at the level of defined roles and responsibilities. We were formed as a team due to the decisions of the board in hiring me to be the team leader (president). Forming was defined by general principles and practices for serving together in fulfillment of our shared ministry to our geographic region.

Norming

During the norming stage, the team interacts with one another according to a set of written and unwritten rules. A team covenant is agreed on, and values are established to guide the team. When norms are reached, the team leader must adopt a supporting style of leadership, allowing the norms to guide the team in a powerful, unspoken manner.

One of the first items we tackled together as the Vision New England team was a set of personnel policies and procedures. Stating my expectations for written staff reports and detailed expense reports was reflective of my earlier years of ministry in the local church setting. The team embraced these practices as good, workable ideas, and they complemented the direction we were heading in the reorganization of the ministry. By consensus we agreed to make these our policy. There were several team members absent from the discussions, however, and their disapproval eventually emerged.

Storming

As team members begin to work together, problems crop up inevitably. During the storming stage, members will challenge and question the team leader. Some call this the "shoot-the-leader" stage due to the many questions that come up, such as, Is our purpose the right one? Are we on the right track? Are we making progress? The leader's job is to coach, encourage, and reassure the team members. A coaching style of leadership is helpful during this stage of the team's development. To build an interdependent team, members need a lot of emotional, spiritual, and personal support during this stormy period, and leaders must be comfortable with some conflict and challenges. Particularly crucial are the leader's listening and coaching skills.

The storming stage occurred within the first six months of my tenure at Vision New England. The issue that embroiled the staff team was the personnel policies we had "agreed to" earlier, but the most specific dissent came out as we discussed our fund-raising philosophies. Some on the team wanted to follow a George Mueller approach, meaning only pray and never overtly ask the constituents for money. Others wanted to make strong written and verbal appeals. Still others wanted to slowly build our financial footing through events and campaigns, attracting new donors with activities that would draw them into our fellowship. We stormed our way through these discussions until we came to a mutual decision to use a variety of approaches, not exclusively a single method. It was a creative solution to which we all agreed. The storming stage drew us closer to one another and we became a much stronger team as a result.

While many fear the storming stage and want to avoid it at all costs, it is a stage that every team will experience and must confront head-on. When it's handled prayerfully, lovingly, and respectfully, a ministry team will experience great growth and maturity. Strong and loving leadership is an essential ingredient for weathering the storm.

Performing

During this stage, the team members begin to fulfill tasks by producing shared work. A team leader can settle into more of a delegating style of leadership during this phase, which will allow more time for analyzing and planning for the future. By delegating, the leader turns over responsibility and authority for decision making and problem solving to the team members. This is the most fruitful and productive phase of team development and displays the maturity of the ministry team like no other stage.

During the high-performance stages of our team's development at Vision New England, we were creatively handling all of our major conflicts, making strategic decisions, fostering healthy relationships among the team, growing substantially in financial resources, building a new ministry home, adding depth and strength to our team, and serving our constituency with excellence. There's nothing like a high-performing team.

Like a well-oiled machine, there is no stopping it from freely moving forward with high speed and great spiritual intensity.

Sustaining the growth and development of a mature team is an ongoing challenge, because inevitably the complexion of the team will change, and when new people join the team and do not share the same values for team development, the team can begin to unravel. What was once a strong and vibrant team can slowly erode and become ineffective. When this happens, the leadership of the team needs to recognize the fundamental team values that first brought them together and begin all over again in developing a team through all the life stages noted above.

Becoming a Healthy Team

The materials in this text are a distillation of a variety of excellent resources available today (several are noted in the bibliography) as well as a compilation of my own study and work with people in a vast array of ministry team settings. I applaud the work of my colleagues in team development and have learned extensively from them. The focus of this book, however, is to offer a memorable acronym for teams that embodies the maxims for healthy team life and ministry service. Each of the five main traits of a healthy team has four sub-traits that support and define it, identifying the realistic challenges of leading ministry teams today. Again, when a team is healthy, it will:

Trust
Empower
Assimilate
Manage
Serve

When teams don't embody these basic traits, they are merely working groups that look more like a poorly managed circus than a high-performing team.

A Team Prayer

Lord of our ministry team, we entrust our hearts into your hands this day. We know that there have been several times when we have entered the team experience with many other selfish interests distracting our attention from our central mission, ministry, and message. Help us to become your faithful disciples, who look out first for the interests of others before attending to our own needs. Help us to listen intently to one another and serve each other as members of the same team. Lead us onward in our pursuit of commonly shared concerns. We delight to serve you together, we are thrilled that you have led us to one another, we look forward to how you will enhance our experiences, and we trust you to lead us every step of the way. Help us to become a healthier team, fully equipped to embody the vision you have given to us. May the joy of the Lord be our daily strength and may what we say and do together bring a smile to your heart, O Lord. Watch over and protect our team, for your honor and glory and for the furthering of the work of your kingdom. In the name of God the Father, Son, and Holy Spirit, the perfected and united TEAM. Amen.

For Reflection

1. Is your team functioning today more like a work group or like a team? In what ways is this being evidenced?
2. From the definition of a healthy ministry team, identify in which of the key components your team is strongest and weakest. Why is this?
3. In what stage of life is your team today (infancy, childhood, adolescence, adulthood, or maturity) and how is this demonstrated?
4. Has your team experienced a "storm" and in what ways did you handle the storm appropriately (or inappropriately)? What lessons were learned or still need to be considered?
5. What does your team need to do this coming month to become a more effective, higher-performing team?

3

Healthy Teams Trust

Tim didn't know he had a pit bull on his team when he first met Rick. In fact, at first, the pit bull was more like a loveable collie or golden retriever. For several years, Tim and Rick had a wonderful relationship. Rick admired Tim's leadership and regularly expressed his gratitude through dozens of written notes and lots of public praise. Rick aspired to Tim's abilities as a leader and generously shared his interest in learning from Tim by remaining on his team. He was one of Tim's strongest supporters.

When Tim moved from one ministry to the next within the context of his local church and an area parachurch ministry, Rick followed him, wanting to continue to serve on Tim's teams. This lasted for more than two decades until one season of service dimmed the lights on what was previously a bright and promising ministry relationship. Much to Tim's surprise, the Judas or betrayer side of Rick became blatantly apparent in dark and difficult ways.

Rick had become a member of Tim's overseeing council at the local parachurch ministry where Tim was serving as team leader. Since Rick had been known to be an advocate of Tim's for several years, they were a force to be reckoned with in the context of the ministry, having served together on several short-term special assignments and on a few sub-committees of the council. They saw eye to eye on virtually every major decision and were enthusiastically supportive of one another throughout their tenure of service.

This was true until one decision Tim made sent Rick through the roof. Tim had the courage to stand up against an unprincipled decision made by another local parachurch ministry that was led by one of Rick's relatives. Rick's vicious pit bull tendencies came out in full force on this one! It wasn't until much later that Tim discovered Rick's discontent. In the meantime, behind the scenes, Rick was plotting for Tim's removal from the team and causing a great deal of discord. Tim eventually left that ministry and the conflict was never resolved.

If it hadn't been for a handful of faithful Barnabas-like colleagues who circled around Tim and encouraged him, his years of service might have ended. They came alongside him to offer prayers, love, wise counsel, and support. They poured courage into his tired heart and this sustained him with renewed energy. They reminded him of the gifts and abilities God had richly granted to him and of the bright and promising future yet ahead of him. Standing with him throughout the long, drawn-out ordeal, they were his source of strength in the midst of a difficult relational catastrophe.

Tim and Rick's experience is multiplied over and over again in many ministry settings today. The details of the story vary according to the particular situation, but the narrative accounts are very similar as scores of worn-out team leaders repeat them. These faithful servants have tirelessly given heart, soul, mind, body, and spirit to local church and parachurch ministry settings. They have made countless decisions, led myriad ministry endeavors, served side by side with untold numbers of team members, and daily exercised their calling as leaders and members of ministry teams worldwide. Then, all of a sudden, often out of the blue, they get sideswiped by a Judas who shows up and tries to discredit them. For a variety of reasons, this person appears on the scene to disrupt the flow of mission, ministry, or message, and all hell (forgive the use of the word here, but if we're telling the truth about teams, that's truly what it feels like!) breaks loose among the team. Any trust that once existed is gone. Broken trust leads to suspicion and ultimately to destruction (unless of course an effective means of conflict resolution is found—the only hope for rebuilding trust among teams. I will deal with this later in this chapter).

The Key to Health

Without trust there is no team. There is no effective service. There is no quality of life together. There is little blessing from God. Trust is the starting point for all healthy relationships, the fuel for team ministry, and the cornerstone of group effectiveness. When trust is breached and left unrepaired, relationships are destroyed and Christian witness diminished. Trust that is broken and left unresolved is the nastiest, most catastrophic, and most destructive force fighting against team effectiveness.

Tim and Rick experienced trust busting at its worst. Their mutual trust had been built over decades of relationship vitality. Because so much equity had been invested in their friendship and partnership in ministry, the break was especially disastrous. Not only did the two of them experience relational fallout, but the ministry they were once serving together limped along weakly after that.

In 1 Corinthians 12:12, 24–25 the apostle Paul reminds us: "The *team* is a unit, though it is made up of many parts; and though all its parts are many, they form one *team*. So it is with Christ. . . . But God has combined the members of the *team* and has given greater honor to the parts that lacked it, so that there should be no division in the *team*." Oneness, unity, and honor are the bases of the trust that exists on healthy teams. When any one of these does not exist, the team will suffer. Tim and Rick had these at one point but lost them almost overnight.

When we honor one another in a spirit of unity and oneness, we are embodying the basis for trusting relationships. The "one anothers" in the Scriptures are further descriptors of the kind of community within teams that God delights to impart to his people. We need to submit to his love and lordship in our individual lives and invite the empowering presence of God's Spirit into our shared experiences as a team. These "one anothers" are expressions of love, which in turn build trust among team members:

- Love one another (John 13:34–35; Rom. 13:8; 1 Peter 1:22; 1 John 3:11, 23; 4:7, 11–12).
- Confess your sins and pray for one another (James 5:16).
- Care for one another (1 Cor. 12:24–25).
- Greet one another (1 Peter 5:14).
- Bear one another's burdens (Gal. 6:2).
- Encourage and build up one another (1 Thess. 5:11; Heb. 3:13; 10:25).
- Submit to one another (Eph. 5:21).
- Bear with one another and forgive one another (Eph. 4:2; Col. 3:13).
- Admonish one another (Col. 3:16).
- Serve one another in love (Gal. 5:13).
- Spur one another on toward love and good deeds (Heb. 10:24).

Teams that embody the "one anothers" are teams that long to fulfill the mandate of oneness, unity, and honor spelled out so clearly in 1 Corinthians 12. The one anothers need to be practiced regularly within the context of relational ministry. They are attributes of team health that are not learned by osmosis. Holding each other mutually accountable to living out these community-building truths will significantly enhance your work and witness.

Thankfully for Tim, when his fallout with Rick occurred, he had other team relationships that were filled with trust and these people became his "Barnabas" encouragers. Tim turned to them in his time of dismay, and they began to express and embody the one anothers described above. He was cared for, loved, encouraged, and served in tangible and intangible ways. Team members who were aware of the situation offered to pray regularly with Tim and urged him to respond to the crisis in ways that honored and pleased God. They circled around him and sustained him, preparing him for future ministry service in several subsequent and much healthier settings. Unfortunately, no one was willing to confront Rick, and his unhealthy pattern of interacting with others continues to this day.

In his book *The Five Dysfunctions of a Team*, Patrick Lencioni offers the following descriptors of how team members express an absence of trust.[1]

- They conceal their weaknesses and mistakes from one another.
- They hesitate to ask for help or provide constructive feedback.
- They hesitate to offer help outside their own areas of responsibility.
- They jump to conclusions about the intentions and aptitudes of others without attempting to clarify them.
- They fail to recognize and tap into one another's skills and experiences.
- They waste time and energy managing their behaviors for effect.
- They hold grudges.
- They dread meetings and find reasons to avoid spending time together.

On the other hand, Lencioni spells out how members of trusting teams embody healthy relationships.

- They admit weaknesses and mistakes.
- They ask for help.
- They accept questions and input about their areas of responsibility.

- They give one another the benefit of the doubt before arriving at a negative conclusion.
- They take risks in offering feedback and assistance.
- They appreciate and tap into one another's skills and experiences.
- They focus time and energy on important issues not politics.
- They offer and accept apologies without hesitation.
- They look forward to meetings and other opportunities to work as a group.

Trust God—Trust One Another

Trusting God is the first and foremost priority for every member of a team and for the team collectively. Healthy ministry teams acknowledge that without an ever-deepening trust in God's provisions, there will never be team oneness, unity, and honor. What does it mean to trust God alone and together?

As a member of the team, when I am trusting God, I am prioritizing my relationship with Christ; I am growing in my understanding of the Word of God, the Holy Bible; I am disciplining myself to be prayerful in my daily times of peaceful solace; and I am reflecting on the gifts that come from the hand of God and expressing heartfelt gratitude to the Father for his unconditional expressions of love. In essence, I am learning to put my complete trust in a loving God who invites me into his intimate fellowship. My trust as a member of the team is holistic; it fully encompasses every aspect of my personal life and is in concert with where I am today and where God is leading me in the future.

Each member who trusts God with his or her whole heart is entering the team experience as a person who is on the road to becoming a healthy disciple.[2] The healthy disciple is prayerful in all aspects of personal life and ministry and relies on God's power and the authority of the Word. Here are ten traits of a healthy disciple:

1. *The healthy disciple experiences God's empowering presence.* He or she understands the role of the Holy Spirit and lives daily with a fresh reality of his power and presence. "The Counselor, the Holy Spirit, will teach you all things and will remind you of everything I have said to you" (John 14:26).

2. *The healthy disciple engages in God-exalting worship.* He or she participates wholeheartedly in meaningful, God-focused, congregational worship experiences on a weekly basis. "The true worshipers will worship the Father in spirit and truth, for they are the kind of worshipers the Father seeks" (John 4:23).

3. *The healthy disciple practices the spiritual disciplines.* He or she pursues spiritual disciplines, including prayer, Bible study, and reflection, daily in quietness and solitude. "Remain in me, and I will remain in you" (John 15:4).

4. *The healthy disciple learns and grows in community.* He or she is involved in spiritual and relational growth in the context of a safe and affirming group of like-minded believers. Jesus' disciples experienced community in miraculous ways when they listened together for the voice of the Savior. "When they did [obey Jesus], they were unable to haul the net in because of the large number of fish" (John 21:6).

5. *The healthy disciple commits to loving and caring relationships.* He or she prioritizes the qualities of relational vitality that lead to genuine love for one another in the home, workplace, church, and community. "My command is this: Love each other as I have loved you. Greater love has no one than this, that he lay down his life for his friends" (John 15:12–13).

6. *The healthy disciple exhibits Christ-like servanthood.* He or she practices being a servant in every relational context

of life and ministry. "I have set you an example that you should do as I have done for you" (John 13:15).

7. *The healthy disciple shares the love of Christ generously.* He or she maximizes every opportunity to share the love of Christ in word and deed with those outside the faith. "For God so loved the world that he gave his one and only Son, that whoever believes in him shall not perish but have eternal life" (John 3:16).

8. *The healthy disciple manages life wisely and with account-ability.* He or she develops personal life-management skills and lives within a web of accountable relationships. "As long as it is day, we must do the work of him who sent me" (John 9:4).

9. *The healthy disciple networks with the body of Christ.* He or she makes an effort to reach out to others within the Christian community for relationships, worship, prayer, fellowship, and ministry. "May they be brought to complete unity to let the world know that you sent me and have loved them even as you have loved me" (John 17:23).

10. *The healthy disciple stewards a life of abundance.* He or she recognizes that every resource comes from the hand of God and is to be used generously for kingdom priorities and purposes. "Unless a kernel of wheat falls to the ground and dies, it remains only a single seed. But if it dies, it produces many seeds" (John 12:24).

When a team is growing in their collective trust of God, they are first and foremost encouraging each member to become a healthy disciple. It's essential that each member of the team learn how to trust God, discern his loving voice, and follow obediently after his gracious will. Holding each other accountable to growth in Christlikeness assists each team member in his or her pursuit of healthy discipleship. The individual initiatives toward righteousness will have positive ripple effects on the abundant life, health, and vitality of the team.

Build Trust through Community

In addition to individual team members deepening their spiritual vitality, the healthy team grows *together* in their trust of God. This happens as individual members come to the team within the context of their own personal spiritual development, having a heart's desire to see each member of the team grow spiritually. As the team meets together, the quality of their shared spiritual experience is the apex of their gatherings.

We saw this community established in the early church and recorded for us in the book of Acts. For example:

> They devoted themselves to the apostles' teaching and to the fellowship, to the breaking of bread and to prayer. Everyone was filled with awe, and many wonders and miraculous signs were done by the apostles. All the believers were together and had everything in common. Selling their possessions and goods, they gave to anyone as he had need. Every day they continued to meet together in the temple courts. They broke bread in their homes and ate together with glad and sincere hearts, praising God and enjoying the favor of all the people. And the Lord added to their number daily those who were being saved.
>
> Acts 2:42–47

It was one thing for individuals to be growing as a result of the apostles' teaching, but it was the fellowship, breaking of bread, and prayer that led them into awe, wonder, and miraculous accomplishments shared within, among, and as a result of their community. The first-century disciples became the first Christian ministry team following the life of Jesus. They experienced so much together—joyful exuberance, bitter disappointment, and everything in between. When the team was united most significantly, it was when their distinctives as Christians were most evident, as expressed in places like Acts 2 noted above. It's time for ministry teams to return to our biblical roots!

Let's recall our definition of a healthy team:

A Christian ministry team is a manageable group of diversely gifted people who hold one another accountable to serve joyfully together for the glory of God by:

- sharing a common mission
- embodying the loving message of Christ
- accomplishing a meaningful ministry
- anticipating transformative results

A *Christian* ministry team is not Christian in name only. When we describe ourselves as Christians we need to talk and live and serve as faithful disciples of Jesus Christ. To be a Christian ministry team means that we prioritize what Christ prioritizes—individually and collectively. Christ longs for an intimate relationship with his children, and he prays that we will experience the same among ourselves (John 17). This intimacy should be our number one mission in our personal lives and in our service together as a team.

When the Leadership Transformations, Inc., board of directors was first established in July 2003, we set out to become a *trusting* Christian ministry team. We knew that for that to become our reality, we needed to make some fundamental decisions about what we value as a team.

The first priority of our team is to maintain the discipline of sharing our spiritual lives with one another. When we meet as a team, our first order of "business" is to hear about our spiritual journeys. We read and pray through the same devotional materials individually, so that, when we arrive at a meeting, we are talking about readings and prayers and topics that we have previously discovered in our individual devotional experiences. Without parallel, this single decision has become the glue that helps our team experience unprecedented unity.

We tend to spend between 30 and 50 percent of our meeting time caring for the health of each other's soul. We share with one another about how God is at work in our lives, what we are learning from God's Word, how we are developing a life of prayer and reflection, where we find ourselves encouraged or discouraged, how we would like to be prayed for, and what's concerning us at home, work, or in our community. For the LTi leadership team, this has become the most essential ingredient for our team development and ministry effectiveness. We recognize that everything of value will come out of these shared experiences, and we have determined together to never turn back.

In addition to spending a large block of time at each monthly meeting in prayer, sharing, and spiritual nurture, we also go on retreat together. These overnights are set apart for relationship building, worship, prayer, sharing, and planning. When we prioritize our spiritual formation exercises ahead of our planning, we sense afresh God's abiding presence and direction. The decisions we need to make come with swift and seamless unity, even when we don't agree. Most important, the leading of the Holy Spirit builds our common unity for the days ahead. Trust is deepened like never before, and our commitment to one another is solidified.

We also purpose to attend our ministry events with others who are interested in spiritual formation, ensuring that the spiritual needs of our "constituents" are being met. This helps us see with greater clarity that the ministry God has led us to build is in fact being significantly used of the Lord in the hearts and lives of others. When we come back to the board table after these experiences, there is a new depth to our conversations, prayers, and deliberations. Over and above our monthly meetings, ministry offerings, and board retreats, friendships have been formed around each other's dinner tables and in occasional, casual times of fellowship outside the routines of ministry development.

Far too many ministry teams lean heavily on *Robert's Rules of Order* instead of on the Bible's instructions for Christian community. As a result, we tend to treat one another as if we were sitting around a conference table in a local business setting. We start our meetings with a perfunctory prayer and short Bible reading but proceed to spend 95 percent of our time talking at one another about issues and decisions, most of which could have been delegated to others not on the board or to the staff. Most members of such teams find themselves bored, discouraged, or disillusioned about the work of the church or the ministry when the meetings they attend have this sense of corporate orderliness without any sense of the Spirit's presence.

Don't read me wrong. I believe in orderliness, and I think *Robert's Rules of Order* contains the best set of procedural guidelines for meeting effectiveness. But when rules, which smack of a corporate mentality, supercede biblical community and the development of a trusting team, it's best to suspend them and push them to the periphery of a team's shared experiences.

The Leadership Transformations board spends the first third of a meeting with spiritual formation as our core focus. No need for Robert's Rules when it comes to community building through sharing, prayer, worship, Bible study, and reflection. When we are ready to transition from the care of our souls to the oversight of our shared work, we integrate more of the procedural ground rules that define our organizational excellence. At this time we take action, vote on decisions, deliberate options, brainstorm about the future, and make specific, objective plans—all within the context of our shared experience of becoming a spiritually formed and focused team.

When organizational decisions grow out of a set of trust-filled relationships, God's blessing and direction are virtually guaranteed.

Build Trust through Celebration

Healthy teams not only grow in community with one another, they celebrate the wonderful ways God has brought them together and used them for his glory. Celebrations bring the team together and acknowledge the many ways that God has blessed and multiplied their ministry. Teams can celebrate in any number of creative and recreational venues.

During my local church ministry days, we made sure there were lots of celebrations. One of the all-time favorites was our annual volunteer staff appreciation weekend. This was the time we gave thanks for the outstanding service of the hundreds of people who gave sacrificially of their time, talent, and treasure to make our shared educational ministries a reality each week. The intentional ways we said a hearty thank-you were many and varied. For example:

- Saturday morning bowling party. We rented a local bowling alley and invited volunteer staff to spend a few hours bowling with their ministry partners, friends, spouses, and children. There were lots of laughs, prizes, and fun.
- Saturday evening banquet. We decked out the fellowship hall with balloons and festive party decorations, and we provided a nice meal and program for all team members. The pastoral staff and elders served the meal, modeling servant leadership in their appreciation for the team.
- Sunday morning brochure. We spent the money to design and print a lovely brochure featuring the photos of our volunteer team, including all ministry departments and team members' names.
- Sunday morning acknowledgment and prayer. During each of the three morning services, we invited all team leaders and members to stand up or come down to the front of the sanctuary where they were applauded by their peers and the pastor led in a prayer of blessing and thankfulness.
- Slide show or video production. A few times we produced a visual presentation of team members at work serving others. It was pure joy to see the faces of men, women, and children involved in ministry.
- Tributes, testimonies, and thank-you gifts. During the weekend festivities, we made sure we heard stories of life transformation that occurred because of the faithful service of the team. The tangible gifts we gave to them, albeit small and inexpensive, were heartfelt expressions of thanks and affirmation for a job well done.

Don Morgan, formerly the pastor of First Church of Christ in Wethersfield, Connecticut, understood the importance of such celebrations. He learned this priority from a high school coach, "Doc" Abell. He writes:

> I remember his encouraging us, smiling at us, and always being there to cheer us on! He was the model of a good coach, the kind you wanted to give your best to in return. You wouldn't fail such a man. You had to come through, make that basket, climb that rope, or win that race—for the coach! Why? I learned something from him: what it takes to be on the sidelines, clapping my hands, cheering on the team, and celebrating their every success.

This attitude affected Don Morgan's ability to lead the team of a growing, healthy church. He continues:

> A vital, growing church will have such an atmosphere of enthusiasm, mutual encouragement, and delight in unfolding success. This is an atmosphere to be cultivated and nurtured, for it's the atmosphere that will bring out everyone's best. This is the atmosphere that radiates the joy and faith you have in Christ, and in which the Lord's command to love one another is fulfilled in being together for his cause. This celebrative atmosphere will profoundly affect everyone concerned.[3]

Leaders who make it a priority to regularly celebrate the accomplishments of the team will soon discover an ever-deepening commitment level among all members. Not only will it be meaningful to serve on such a team, it can actually be fun.

Build Trust through Communication

I have yet to find a team that overcommunicates. There are innumerable teams that undercommunicate or inappropriately communicate. Effective communication builds trust in relationships and is an essential ingredient of healthy teams. The success of your team and the level of trust your team will acquire are directly proportionate to how well they communicate—leader to team, among team members, and toward those they serve.

John Maxwell challenges leaders in their communication with these standards:

- Be consistent. Nothing frustrates team members more than leaders who can't make up their minds.
- Be clear. Your team cannot execute if the members don't know what you want. Don't try to dazzle anyone with your intelligence; impress people with your straightforwardness.
- Be courteous. Everyone deserves to be shown respect, no matter what the position or what kind of history you might have with him. By being courteous to your people, you set the tone for the entire organization.

Never forget that because you are the leader, your communication sets the tone for the interaction among your people. Teams always reflect their leaders. And never forget that good communication is never one-way. It should not be top-down or dictatorial. The best leaders listen, invite, and then encourage participation.[4]

Among teammates, Maxwell encourages the following qualities to be exhibited:

- Be supportive . . . Communication that is focused on giving rather than getting takes the team to a whole new level.
- Stay current . . . Teammates who rehash old problems and continually open old wounds don't work together. And if they don't work together, they're sunk.
- Be vulnerable . . . Teams are like little communities, and they develop only when the people in them don't posture with one another.

Teams succeed or fail based on the way that team members communicate with one another.[5]

Communication with and among team members is a continual challenge that must be kept in check. The goal of effective communication is empathy, understanding where each is coming from. This is expressed not only through what we say but in what we mean when we say the words that reflect our heart's desires and concerns. The ability to listen carefully, prayerfully, and lovingly to one another builds the kind of trust that's necessary for healthy teams to exist.

Therefore, it's important that we know one another as members of the team—both inside and outside the ministry setting. In other words, we need to know one another beyond the role(s) we play on the team. We need to know more than each other's names and ministry responsibilities. We need to get to know one another at a heart and soul level of communication. Then, as ministry concerns are voiced, we hear them at a trust level and not merely through the spoken words that are uttered.

John Trent helps us understand the challenges we have in communicating with one another by illustrating how different we are. He gives very simple labels to the types of people we will find on our teams, describing people as lions, otters, golden retrievers, or beavers. He gives the following tips for communicating with these four different people types.[6]

1. When communicating with a *lion* (a person who is ambitious, forceful, decisive, strong willed, independent, and goal-oriented):
   - Be clear, specific, brief, and to the point.
   - Stick to business.
   - Be prepared with support material in a well-organized package.
   - Factors that will create tension or dissatisfaction include: talking about things that are not relevant to the issue, leaving loopholes or cloudy issues, appearing disorganized.
2. When communicating with an *otter* (a person who is magnetic, enthusiastic, friendly, demonstrative, and political):
   - Provide a warm and friendly environment.
   - Don't deal with a lot of details; put them in writing.
   - Ask "feeling" questions to draw out their opinions or comments.
   - Factors that will create tension or dissatisfaction

    include: being curt, cold, or tight-lipped; controlling the conversation; dwelling on facts and figures, alternatives, or abstractions.

3. When communicating with a *golden retriever* (a person who is patient, predictable, reliable, steady, relaxed, and modest):
   - Begin with a personal comment; break the ice.
   - Present your case softly, in a nonthreatening manner.
   - Ask "how" questions to draw out their opinions.
   - Factors that will create tension or dissatisfaction include: rushing headlong into business, being domineering or demanding, forcing them to respond quickly to your objectives.

4. When communicating with a *beaver* (a person who is dependent, neat, conservative, perfectionist, careful, and compliant):
   - Prepare your case in advance.
   - Stick to business.
   - Be accurate and realistic.
   - Factors that will create tension or dissatisfaction include: being giddy, casual, informal, or loud; pushing too hard or being unrealistic with deadlines; being disorganized or messy.

Every team has at least one lion, otter, golden retriever, and beaver. It's incumbent on us as leaders and team members to identify ourselves within this simple grid and develop effective ways of communicating with one another. In an atmosphere of loving trust, using such a model can make team building fun, energetic, and creative. And it can diminish unnecessary disagreements simply because we've learned how to communicate and truly hear each other when we speak.

Inevitably, however, every team will experience a breakdown in communication. Trust will be shaken, tried, and tested. The questions remain: How mature will your team be in handling the conflicts that come your way? Will you do so with strength of character, or will you, like Tim and Rick (and countless other teams), allow the conflict to be swept under the carpet or left unattended or treated in an inappropriate manner and ultimately left unresolved?

Build Trust through Conflict

A team's trust is not built only in community, celebration, and communication, but even in times of conflict. All the very best relationships in marriage, family life, friendships, business, and ministry are built through conflict. It's in the crucible of conflict that the refiner's fire matures relationships. It's when conflicts are resolved that strength and stability are created in relationships. It's through a process of healthy conflict resolution that we learn lessons individually and collectively that chip away at the brittle areas and bring out our very best.

Most teams, however, are poorly led in times of conflict. That was certainly the case for Tim and Rick. The leader of the overseeing council was incapable of bringing resolution to the crisis at hand and allowed Rick to get the upper hand in bullying Tim out of a job. Because of the relational dynamics at play, Rick was the most boisterous, threatening, and convincing, mostly behind Tim's back. The rest of the team were shielded from Tim's perspective and made decisions about the future of the ministry according to the lopsided view Rick had painted for them. This particular conflict was left to linger on for many months until Tim discovered afresh God's redemptive plan for his future—on another team.

Teams in general need to learn more about how to resolve conflict. Families of origin are the dominant teacher in how conflicts get resolved. The role models of parents and extended family members are the first influences we have in shaping our understanding of how to handle conflict. In addition, when we enter the neighborhood as children, the schoolyard as adolescents, the college scene and young adulthood as students and employees, we experience more examples of conflict resolution (or lack thereof).

When we enter a local church or parachurch ministry setting, we bring to the team a vast array of backgrounds and experiences with conflict, mostly not very positive or effective. As conflicts arise, we respond out of our previous experience, usually considering conflict taboo and longing for it to be simply dismissed or diminished. In these situations we forget that there are real people involved, and if we truly care about them as fellow team members, we should do everything possible to resolve the conflict constructively, creatively, and in a Christ-like manner.

Patrick Lencioni encourages leaders and teams to recognize the differences between productive ideological conflict and destructive fighting and interpersonal politics.

> Ideological conflict is limited to concepts and ideas, and avoids personality-focused, mean-spirited attacks. However, it can have many of the same external qualities of interpersonal conflict—passion, emotion, and frustration—so much so that an outside observer might easily mistake it for unproductive discord. But teams that engage in productive conflict know that the only purpose is to produce the best possible solution in the shortest period of time. They discuss and resolve issues more quickly and completely than others, and they emerge from heated debates with no residual feelings or collateral damage, but with an eagerness and readiness to take on the next important issue.
>
> Ironically, teams that avoid ideological conflict often do so in order to avoid hurting team members' feelings, and then end up encouraging dangerous tension. When team members do not openly debate and disagree about important ideas, they often turn to back-channel personal attacks, which are far nastier and more harmful than any heated argument over issues. It is also ironic that so many people avoid conflict in the name of efficiency, because healthy conflict is actually a time saver. Contrary to the notion that teams waste time and energy arguing, those that avoid conflict actually doom themselves to revisiting issues again and again without resolution.[7]

Healthy teams acknowledge that conflict is actually very productive. It can create strength as can no other experience. In conflict we discover how vital we are in our team relationships. We trust one another and deal openly, candidly, lovingly, and graciously, with an attitude to forgive when necessary and redemptively restore members back in line with God's priorities for fulfilling his mission, ministry, and message.

Lencioni reminds us of the differences between teams that fear conflict and those that approach conflict productively.[8] Teams that fear conflict:

- have boring meetings
- create environments where back-channel politics and personal attacks thrive
- ignore controversial topics that are critical to team success
- fail to tap into all the opinions and perspectives of team members
- waste time and energy with posturing and interpersonal risk management

Whereas, teams that engage in conflict:

- have lively, interesting meetings
- extract and exploit the ideas of all team members
- solve real problems quickly
- minimize politics
- put critical topics on the table for discussion

So what will it be—a team that embraces the lessons learned through grace, mercy, forgiveness, and healthy conflict resolution or a team that avoids conflict like the plague? It's your choice. Just be sure to pray and ask God first. Trusting God and one another is the cornerstone of a healthy team.

A Team Prayer

Lord of our team, we invite your presence and power to reign supreme in our shared life and ministry. We long to fulfill your mission, ministry, and message through the unique and transformative call you have given to us. We want more than anything to

*trust you with our heart, soul, mind, and strength. And we want
to learn how to trust one another. Help us to build our team on
the principles of community, celebration, communication, and
conflict in ways that bring joy to your heart. Holy Spirit, empower
us with the resolve necessary to do this in ways that bring you
glory. We recognize that building trust is inherent in developing
the quality and essence of our life together. We ask for a fresh
resolve and a bold determination to keep these priorities before
us. Allow us to experience the richness of our common unity and
the joy of our ever-deepening trust. For the sake of Christ and his
kingdom we pray. Amen.*

For Reflection

1. Do you agree that without trust there is no team? Why or why not?
2. What words best describe the current trust level of your team?
3. How can you encourage your team members to deepen their trust in God? Discuss ways in which trust in God impacts the trust level that exists among team members.
4. Dialogue with team members about how the following ways of building trust can be enhanced within your team experiences:

   - community
   - celebration
   - communication
   - conflict

5. What skill does your team need the most in learning how to resolve conflict? How will you begin to address that need in the coming weeks?

4

Healthy Teams Empower

During the week of John F. Kennedy's assassination, Alice began working for the Defense Contract Audit Agency. From November 1963 until June 1983, she worked faithfully as the regional director's administrative assistant. She flourished in her work and thought all along that she would be a government employee for the rest of her career.

We had other ideas in mind for Alice. The Christian Education team at Grace Chapel enjoyed working with Alice as one of our faithful administrative team volunteers. As a member of the church, she was generous with her time and talent and willingly supported the ongoing development of our shared work. We saw in Alice not only tremendous gifts and abilities that enhanced our ministry to children but a humble and gentle heart.

In June 1983 Alice joined the team as my administrative assistant in children's ministry. She remains today, representing one of the best personnel decisions I made in my nearly three decades of ministry service. Alice is known as one of the most valuable players on the staff team at Grace Chapel, assisted by her husband, Tracy, who accompanies her to the office every day to volunteer his services and accomplish any task he's asked to complete. They are unsung heroes in the life of the church and make more ministry happen on a weekly basis than many others in their field. It's been a blessing to watch Alice thrive in her ministry responsibilities as she's weathered with grace, wisdom, and genuine joy the challenges of multiple changes over the years.

The Holy Spirit has empowered Alice to fulfill her daily routines as an administrative assistant. She's been allowed the freedom to use her gifts and abilities in her ministry context. With her natural gifting, she has faithfully executed her job with vitality and seen how God has used her for his greater glory.

Alice rarely complains about the myriad administrative details she must attend to in the children's ministry office (under the tutelage of the children's pastor and in partnership with a small army of volunteers). Her responsibilities include the management of budgets, calendars, events, lists, supplies, equipment, materials, facilities, and curriculum, and she assists in recruiting more than 275 volunteers to work in ongoing children's ministry programs throughout the year.

Ask Alice what is the greatest satisfaction of her role and she will talk about watching children grow up in Christ through ministries like Sunday school and vacation Bible school. She'll tell you about families she has stayed in touch with over the years and how the children she helped to nurture in their faith are now married with their own children. She beams with radiant joy at the thought of helping and supporting volunteer staff members who have become more effective in their work with children.

One of the decisions our team made early on in our development was that every member of the team would be empowered to fulfill their responsibilities. The worst thing to do to another team member is to give him or her a job without the accompanying authority to perform it. If the supervision of Alice included watching over her shoulder, micromanaging her work, or in any way expressing a lack of trust in her abilities, we would have lost her long ago. One of the key issues for

Alice was being entrusted with ever-increasing responsibility and sensing ever-deepening trust in her ability to execute her duties. With impeccable integrity she has earned the trust of leaders and colleagues, and as a result she has flourished in her accomplishments. She is a role model to many, including the author of this book.

What does it take to empower members of our teams in healthy ways? What does God want from leaders as we look to the Father's way of dealing with his children? How are we to embody leadership *and* followership that builds on trust and leads all team members into deeper fulfillment and God-honoring empowerment? What does the analogy of the body in 1 Corinthians 12 teach us about empowerment?

The Body—United and Empowered

Two verses in 1 Corinthians 12 are empowerment verses:

- For we were all baptized by one Spirit into one *team*—whether Jews or Greeks, slave or free—and we were all given the one Spirit to drink (v. 13).
- Its parts should have equal concern for each other (v. 25).

The apostle Paul is reminding us here that whether we are formerly from Jewish or Greek (Gentile) background, slave or free, each one who has received the gifting and empowerment of the Spirit is a part of the team. We are to see in one another an equal concern for the essential parts we play, and in the Spirit's power, we become united as a body. This is a simple yet profound truth.

Having equal concern for Jews and Greeks, for slaves and free was a radical thought to the believers in the early church. This idea may be no big deal to the reader today, but to the recipient of Paul's message in Corinth, it had huge ramifications.

Paul loved the church in Corinth, where he served for a year and a half. He preached in the synagogue with great success, despite the stubborn hostility of the Jews there (Acts 18:1–17). He had deep insights into the culture of Corinth and was very concerned about the struggling development of the church, which led to his writing the Corinthian letters when he was in Ephesus.

Corinth was a populous city with one of the most lucrative commercial trades in the ancient world, and it was known for its wickedness and debauchery. This was a city filled with people who lived evil, reckless, riotous lives. There were native Greek citizens, as well as those of Roman descent, Phoenicians and Phrygians from the east, and many Jews.

From the outset of the letter, the apostle Paul addresses his concerns "to those sanctified in Christ Jesus and called to be holy" (1 Cor. 1:2). This is followed by his expressions of love for the people in Corinth:

> I always thank God for you because of his grace given you in Christ Jesus. For in him you have been enriched in every way—in all your speaking and in all your knowledge—because our testimony about Christ was confirmed in you. Therefore you do not lack any spiritual gift as you eagerly wait for our Lord Jesus Christ to be revealed. He will keep you strong to the end, so that you will be blameless on the day of our Lord Jesus Christ. God, who has called you into fellowship with his Son Jesus Christ our Lord, is faithful.
>
> verses 4–9

On the heels of his expressions of love and thankfulness, he launches into his deepest distress—their divisions. His appeal is for their unity despite their differences. He writes: "I appeal to you, brothers, in the name of our Lord Jesus Christ, that all of you agree with one another so that there may be no divisions among you and that you may be perfectly united in mind and thought. . . . What I mean is this: One of you says, 'I follow Paul'; another, 'I follow Apollos'; another, 'I follow Cephas'; still another, 'I follow Christ'" (vv. 10, 12). What he is referring to is their allegiances:

- To those who claim to follow Paul, he is addressing the Gentiles.
- To those who claim to follow Apollos, he is speaking to the intellectuals who were turning Christianity into a philosophy rather than a religion.
- To those who claim to follow Cephas, he is addressing the Jews who taught that a believer must still observe the Jewish law.
- To those who claim to follow Christ, he is most likely describing a small, intolerant, self-righteous group who were claiming to be the only true Christians in Corinth.[1]

Paul continues in the first chapter of the letter to place additional emphasis on the rift that was apparent among the various factions of the faith. In verses 23 and 24, he continues: "We preach Christ crucified: a stumbling block to Jews and foolishness to Gentiles, but to those whom God has called, both Jews and Greeks, Christ the power of God and the wisdom of God."

The gospel of Christ was a stumbling block to the Jews because it was too incredible to conceive of God's chosen One ending his life on a cross. And it was folly to the Greeks because they could not imagine a God who would empathize with humanity so deeply that he would involve himself in human affairs and heartfelt needs. The Jews were looking for startling signs of the Messiah's coming. The Greeks were seeking wisdom and mental mastery of the magnificent. The form of God in Christ was foreign to both.

Over and over again Paul speaks to the divisions in the church. Even immediately prior to the twelfth chapter, we see him reinforcing his concerns when he speaks to the reader about the Lord's Supper. He says, "In the following directives [about the Lord's supper] I have no praise for you. . . . there are divisions among you. . . . [Therefore] a man ought to examine himself before he eats of the bread and drinks of the cup" (vv. 17, 18, 28).

His obvious concern was for the believers in Corinth to be united despite their differences. He urged them to be all that God intended when he created them with their unique characteristics and ethnicities. In addition, he called them to grow, being continually sanctified as gifted and empowered members of his body—the Church of God in Corinth.

It didn't matter to Paul if they were of Greek or Jewish descent, if they were slave or free, male or female. What mattered most for Paul is that they knew Christ and that they were united in Christ. The unity amid their diversity is what would strengthen the church. The empowerment of the people to become all that God intended for them is what would lead to their growth, health, and vitality. Those same intentions are what God wants for us as twenty-first-century believers.

The Body—Appropriately Gifted

The apostle Paul calls for the Corinthian believers not only to be united and empowered in, by, and through their uniqueness but to acknowledge and affirm the appropriate ways God has gifted them as individual members of the body. In the first eleven chapters he has been building up to this point, dealing with Christ the unifier, the Spirit as their source of wisdom, the faithfulness of servant-apostles, how to deal with expelling an immoral brother, lawsuits among believers, sexual immorality, marriage, idols, freedom, and worship. Paul is speaking to their divisiveness and leading them into a higher place of integrity in their walk of faith together.

About spiritual gifts he doesn't want them ignorant (1 Cor. 12:1). So the chapter begins with Paul once again talking about differences. The previous chapters dealt with differences in ethnicity, sexuality, and religious backgrounds and with differences of opinion on legal matters, idolatry, worship, and religious liberty. Now he jumps into the different ways we are gifted by the Spirit and empowered in our service.

Obviously Paul is concerned that those with differing gifts be handled appropriately. He places extraordinary emphasis on this in verses 4–7 and 11: "There are different kinds of gifts, but the same Spirit. There are different kinds of service, but the same Lord. There are different kinds of working, but the same God works all of them in all men. Now to each one the manifestation of the Spirit is given for the common good . . . all these are the work of one and the same Spirit, and he gives them to each one, just as he determines."

Gifts are given appropriately by the Spirit in differing and unique ways. The list here is diverse: message of wisdom; message of knowledge, faith, healing, miraculous powers, prophecy, distinguishing between spirits, speaking in different kinds of tongues, interpretation of tongues. Elsewhere (for example, in Rom. 12:4–8) Paul adds to the list of diverse gifts in the body, such as prophesying, serving, teaching, encouraging, contributing to the needs of others, leadership, and mercy. Albeit not exhaustive, these lists express the diversity of gifts found in the complexity of the body of Christ—in the first-century as well as in the twenty-first-century church.

In all of this, Paul is setting the stage for his portrayal of the body as his metaphor for what the church in Corinth was to strive toward as a divided church. In preparing his readers for this passage, Paul is continuing his thematic focus of unity in the diversity of the body. He knows that for the church to come together, each member needs to acknowledge the value of all members who make up the community of faith—and make sure all are empowered to serve the church in their uniquely God-given ways.

The church in Corinth was appropriately gifted so that their unity would be strengthened. As each member of the diverse body of believers was individually gifted, they were to share their gifts within the context of the church. When this occurred, the church would be united and the members fully prepared to serve side by side for the sake of the gospel of Christ. As it was then, so must it now and forever be!

Let's look again at our definition of a healthy team:

A Christian ministry team is *a manageable group of diversely gifted people* who hold one another accountable to serve joyfully together for the glory of God by:

- sharing a common mission
- embodying the loving message of Christ
- accomplishing a meaningful ministry
- anticipating transformative results

The emphasis in this chapter is to understand that a healthy team builds on the trust factor, described in the previous chapter, and then empowers one another to fully express his or her uniquely distinct contribution to the body of Christ. This is done within a manageably sized group of team members who get to know and affirm what they see emerging in one another's hearts and lives. When this occurs, unity in diversity is achieved and ministry to others flows out from their very being.

Alice's empowerment emerged over several months as the team observed how God had gifted her for ministry and what her place on the team would be. She was in a support role administratively, but her place on the team was of equal importance to the rest. She stood out in her uniqueness, not in her superiority. As others affirmed her, she developed her abilities and expressed her giftedness with ever-increasing clarity and effectiveness. Together as a team, we were able to affirm in Alice her

- *Story.* We heard her share her journey and we celebrated the many ways God had prepared her for the ministry she now enjoyed.
- *Voice.* We were encouraged by the ways she interacted with others with growing courage and conviction of heart and mind.
- *Call.* We honored the ways in which God had brought her to our team "for such a time as this," and we affirmed the role she played on the team through her Holy Spirit–empowered life.

Empower through Gifts and Passions

"God doesn't want you to settle for anything less than His very best," writes Pastor Wayne Cordeiro. "You have been created with special talents, abilities and gifts. That's wonderful in itself, but what's even more important is how you invest those qualities. You must discover and develop your talents, abilities and gifts to their fullest potential; only then will you be able to crash through your barriers of limitation."[2]

Pastor Cordeiro and his team at New Hope Christian Fellowship in Honolulu, Hawaii, have created a course to help others find their gifts and passions. DESIGN is an acrostic that stands for the different ingredients that, when combined, provide individual team members with a greater appreciation and understanding of their gifts. Once recognized, they lead an individual to realize his or her full potential in Christ. The following is a summary of the program.[3]

- *D is for desire.* What is your passion? If all things were equal and you could do anything in the world for the Lord, what job would you choose to do? What would make every day feel like Christmas?

- *E is for experience.* Your past experiences are important considerations when seeking and finding your design. What tasks or projects have influenced you in the past? What have you learned from the times when you have been hurt? How have they made you more compassionate toward others in similar situations?

- *S is for spiritual gift.* Every person who knows Jesus Christ is endowed with one or more spiritual gifts. These are enumerated in 1 Corinthians 12, Romans 12, Ephesians 4, and 1 Peter 4. God never intended for Christ's ministry to cease when he ascended into heaven, so he decided that his ministry would be carried on through those who believe. Knowing that we could never do it on our own, God sent his Spirit, who distributed gifts to the church through which we would carry on his work. What are your spiritual gifts? Are you willing for God to use you in any of them?

- *I is for individual style.* Each of us has a unique temperament that we call a personality or individual style. Some of us are more extroverted, while others tend toward being more introverted. Your individual style will not change your calling as a Christian, but it will tell you how to carry out your calling.
- *G is for growth phase.* Each of us is still growing in the Lord. Some of us may be spiritual toddlers, while others are more like adolescents or adults. Some have knowledge but have a long way to go in gaining wisdom. Others are fountains of common sense but know very little of the Bible. Are you an infant, toddler, adolescent, young adult, or a mature adult in your relationship with Christ?
- *N is for natural abilities.* What do you enjoy doing? Do you have a natural talent for fixing things? What about strategic planning, financial planning, working with the elderly, or working with babies? When we minister within our design, life gets exciting and fun. God isn't some unbending drillmaster who demands our service. He really wants our heart! God doesn't want us just to serve him; he wants us to serve him joyfully! Then we will be functioning in the way God designed us to function.

The key to discovering how God designed you in the first place is to seek ways to fulfill that design as members of a healthy team. When we come to a fuller understanding of ourselves, we are better able to serve others. As we grow in the utilization of our gifts, the empowerment of the Spirit of God emerges in ways that reflect the design that God intended all along. There is joy in the process for all who choose to take this step forward in earnest pursuit of their gifts, abilities, passions, dreams, and desires.

Empower through Defined Responsibilities

There's an old story of a rabbi living in a Russian city a century ago. Disappointed by his lack of direction and life purpose, he wandered out into the chilly evening. With his hands thrust deep into his pockets, he aimlessly walked through the empty streets, questioning his faith in God, the Scriptures, and his calling to ministry. The only thing colder than the Russian winter air was the chill within his own soul. He was so enshrouded by his own despair that he mistakenly wandered into a Russian military compound that was off-limits to civilians.

The silence of the evening chill was shattered by the bark of a Russian soldier. "Who are you? And what are you doing here?"

"Excuse me?" replied the rabbi.

"I said, 'Who are you and what are you doing here?'"

After a brief moment the rabbi, in a gracious tone so as not to provoke the soldier, said, "How much do you get paid every day?"

"What does that have to do with you?" the soldier retorted.

With some delight, as though he had just made a discovery, the rabbi said, "I will pay you the equal sum if you will ask me those same two questions every day: Who are you? And what are you doing here?"[4]

There are far too many individuals joining teams today who have no clarity about their own giftedness or what they are called to do on the team. Team leaders must pay close attention to the individuals on the team who are looking for specific answers to basic questions about their roles and responsibilities. A chill of ineffectiveness goes deep within the soul of teams composed of people who don't know what they are supposed to do and are left to figure it out on their own. A healthy team empowers each member of the team, making sure everyone knows his or her role and purpose.

Every person who comes onto a team is asking some very basic questions:

- *What am I supposed to do in the context of the work of our team?*

Be clear in defining roles and responsibilities so that there is little confusion and no overlap in responsibilities for completing the team's ministry.

- *Will the team and team leader allow me to do what's asked of me?*
  Empower each team member to fulfill his or her work in the context of the full team being activated for service.
- *Will the team and team leader provide help when I need it?*
  Be a resource for all members of the team, providing everything they need to accomplish their ministry effectively.
- *Will the team and team leader tell me how I'm doing all along the way?*
  Be affirming and appreciative and provide constructive assistance in areas that need further development or strengthening.

If individual team members are unsure of their gifts and abilities, it's important for the leader and the team to recognize this and help dispel the confusion. There are a number of resources available for this purpose, such as the DESIGN curriculum noted above. One of the first empowering exercises for leaders is to help the members of the team define who they are, how God created them, and the particular gifts and calling they represent. Helping a child of God give voice to his or her call will further this person's ability to live out his or her story in light of God's will.

Empower through Teachability and Resourcing

In all the work I have done with teams over the years, the number one attribute I look for in effective team members is teachability—an openness to continual learning and growth. If a person joins the team and has an attitude that reflects any sense of haughtiness or pride, it will hurt team camaraderie and ultimately damage team effectiveness.

For a moment, let me compare two members of a team I previously led where the contrast was sharp. Rob and Randy joined the team at about the same time. Rob was invited onto the team to teach in the four-year-old department and Randy was the team leader. Randy was highly regarded by his peers for the long-standing influence he had on the entire department. In fact it was one of the few ministry departments for which we never had to worry about recruiting new members. People who loved children flocked to Randy's side.

Rob had heard about Randy's reputation and signed up to teach in his department. Early on, Rob was energetic about the opportunity and was a positive contributor to the team. One week during the large-group teaching session, when Rob filled in for Randy, he made a glaring mistake. He altered the lesson and told the children about what the Lord "had spoken" to him that particular week. Bewildered and confused, the children did not understand any part of the lesson, since it was above their mental capabilities as preschoolers. The other teachers in the classroom were equally confused by Rob's teaching and reported it to Randy.

Trying to understand where Rob was coming from, Randy set up a time to meet with him. Rob was surprised that anyone was concerned. After all, he had "heard from the Lord" and was only doing what he thought it best to do. He defended his treatment of the Scriptures, even though it was a completely different lesson than anyone else had prepared and it was far beyond the young children's comprehension. Rob became adamant about his cause and belligerently decided to take this to a higher authority.

Since I was the pastor in charge of this area of ministry, Rob sought me out. He came to our meeting with a lengthy letter in hand outlining his concern for the lack of spiritual maturity in Randy's department. He used Scripture to defend his actions and his teaching. He belittled those who would disagree with his "word from the Lord" and turned it around as a word of condemnation for the ministry and the leadership. It became a larger-than-life issue for us to manage and it stretched our abilities to know how best to work with Rob in the future. He ultimately left the department, determined to find a more appropriate team for his gifts and abilities.

Rob's difficulty stemmed from theological and practical issues. On both he was immovable and unteachable. It mattered more to him that he was right than that he could learn anything. Though he tried for many years to find his niche in the church, he remained uncooperative in every setting. Everyone who worked with Rob tried to reason with him, but he was not open to any correction. Eventually he was asked not to serve in any leadership role and was sidelined as a result.

It's amazing how many Robs there are in local churches and parachurch ministries today. For some reason, these people believe they were called to be contrary team members. Walking away from the team charter, doing their own thing, or showing passive-aggressive behaviors that destroy teams, they find a strange satisfaction in being difficult. The bottom line is, they aren't teachable.

Who is on your team and how do they reflect a teachable spirit?

- *Wonderful team members* are those who are easy to get along with, helpful, fully engaged, willing to serve, teachable, and servant-hearted in every way. They are pure joy to have around and their presence is empowering!

- *Wandering team members* are those who have a differing view to offer on most issues, tend toward negativity and a complaining spirit, and believe it's their calling in life to offer the downside or contrary opinion for the team to remember. These are the team members who become the high-maintenance ones, exhibit very little teachability, and wear out the leader. They demoralize the team with their negativity and are always inviting others to join them on the prickly path of counterproductivity.

- *Wondering team members* are those who have said yes to join the team but are still a bit suspicious or curious about the team. They still need to be convinced of the mission and need to be empowered to join the center of team life, fully engaging in the work of the team. They are speculating about their contribution to the team, sitting on the sidelines until they are won over either by individuals or by the mission, whichever feeds into their passion and giftedness. Their sense of wonder can be tapped into and their service directed to the team's needs if they have a teachable heart.

In most ministry teams today, the majority of members are *wondering* if there is a meaningful place for them on the team. About 20 percent are *wonderful* and an equal number are *wandering*. What about your team? What can you do to monitor the negative effect of the *wandering* while striving proactively to engage the *wondering* into the team's mission? Utilizing the *wonderful* in this endeavor is the smartest way for team leaders to go; it's nearly impossible to do this on their own.

Most *wondering* team members are actually very teachable. Smart leaders will pay attention to the questions these people raise. Since a teachable spirit can be acquired, it's important that the designated leader understand how to discern and fan the flame in those who seem willing to learn. On the other hand, most *wandering* team members are difficult to draw into the center of team life. For them, the pursuit of their own agenda generally supercedes that of the team. The goal is to broaden the number of *wonderful* team players by drawing in the *wondering* and *wandering* who have a teachable heart.

Teachable team members need to be resourced for action. Resources for team members will vary according to the tasks at hand. Resource needs will generally fall into the following categories:

- Personnel—how many people are needed to accomplish the mission?
- Facilities—what kind of facilities will best accommodate the ministry?
- Programs—what programs are working to resource the needs of the community being served?

- Supplies—what supplies are necessary so that members of the team can function fully in their respective roles and responsibilities?

Answers to these questions will lead to the fulfillment of the resourcing needs of a healthy team.

Empower through Delegation and Accountability

Shortly after the death of T. W. Wilson in May 2001, *Christianity Today* ran a tribute to him and his tireless team efforts with his longtime friend Billy Graham. Wilson did many things for Graham, from managing his personal security to being his traveling companion. He was an extraordinarily important member of the Graham team, mostly because his heart was knit together with Billy and the others. Wilson personified the consistency and longevity of the Graham ministry that led the most phenomenal evangelism campaigns of the twentieth century.

> The team of which T. W. Wilson was a key member has embodied a biblical principle of ministry: the formation of teams under the leading of God's Spirit for mutual encouragement, accountability, and discernment.
>
> Jesus sent out his disciples two by two. Paul traveled and ministered with Silas, Timothy, Barnabas and others. (Paul even shared his byline with Timothy and Silas.) Such team ministry is a divinely ordained prophylactic against a variety of ills, ranging from discouragement to embezzlement.
>
> Of course, there are bad team ministries. Public ministries attract sycophants who bask in reflected glory and feed their parasitic egos off another. And inner circles can create jealousy and division in the ranks. You can always tell a responsible team ministry by the sacrificed ego and mutual subordination.
>
> The sacrifice involved in team ministry recalls what Paul and Timothy wrote to the Philippians: "In lowliness of mind let each esteem the other better than themselves. Look not every man on his own things, but every man also on the things of

others." Paul and Timothy give this advice just before they urge believers to have in themselves the self-abasing mind of Christ. But we cannot help wondering if the team ministry that Paul experienced with his own traveling soul mates in ministry was not also an inspiration for this exhortation.

Any tribute to T. W. Wilson is a tribute to the importance of teams, of shared ministry, and of the mutual accountability of soul mates. The pattern is biblical but rarely realized.[5]

It would have been one thing for Billy Graham to delegate to T. W. meaningful work in their service together. Here, however, the delegation of responsibilities was enhanced by the mutual accountability they enjoyed.

Team members who are delegated tasks without responsibility are limited in their ability to accomplish their jobs. When team members are asked to fulfill a role and a defined duty and are trusted to complete their work without others looking over their shoulder or micromanaging their daily routines, they are empowered. Team leaders and mutually accountable members should be entrusted with much more than a title; they should have meaningful tasks to complete.

Once tasks are delegated, every team member needs to know that he or she will be held accountable to complete the agreed upon assignment. When healthy accountability is in place, team members become exponentially more effective in the full utilization of their gifts, abilities, passions, and calling.

Being accountable to one another is a way of expressing our desire for growth. We open ourselves to the work of God's Spirit in our lives as we entrust the evaluation of our service to the hands and hearts of our co-laborers. In essence we are saying to others that we trust them with their input into our lives. We look forward to learning from our experiences and discovering new ways to tackle issues, programs, and people. Accountability, properly understood and executed, can provide the greatest forum for team maturity. Avoided, it can be a team's downfall.

A team that avoids accountability:

- creates resentment among team members who have different standards of performance;
- encourages mediocrity;
- misses deadlines and key deliverables;
- places an undue burden on the team leader as the sole source of discipline.

A team that holds one another accountable:

- ensures that poor performers feel pressure to improve;
- identifies potential problems quickly by questioning one another's approaches without hesitation;
- establishes respect among team members who are held to the same high standards;
- avoids excessive bureaucracy around performance management and corrective action.[6]

You can choose to become a team that embraces the priority of delegation and healthy accountability, or you can choose to avoid the challenge altogether. The decision you make will determine the future direction of your team and will significantly impact your results. Prayerfully consider the options and walk the high road of empowerment.

A Team Prayer

Loving Father, we thank you for your Spirit's desire to empower us in our service for you and your kingdom. We recognize today that you have gifted us in unique ways. You have fit our team together in a design that reflects your loving will and ways. You have called us to each other and we trust you in the choices you've made that have built us up as a team. Some on the team are wonderful contributors to the ministry, and we thank you especially for their faithfulness. Some are wandering rather aimlessly off the pathway defined for us, and we pray that they will see the light and return to the central mission that binds us together. Some still stand along the perimeter of the team and are watching and waiting for a time when they can dive into our team fellowship and join us with their full hearts. Will you, gracious Father, build our team in ways that honor your Spirit's fresh empowerment, and will you delight to bless our shared endeavors on your behalf? We long to fulfill your loving will and we will praise and thank you for the many ways you entrust your work into our hands. Multiply our individual efforts in a way that pleases you and enlarge our hearts for one another's empowerment as well. We honor you as the Lord of our team and we ask for your power and presence now and always. In the strong name of Jesus we pray. Amen.

For Reflection

1. What does it mean to become fully empowered as a member of a ministry team?
2. In what ways have you been empowered to serve within your gifts and abilities? How are you encouraging this in others?
3. Spend some time reflecting individually and as a team on Wayne Cordeiro's DESIGN outline. What are your desires, experiences, spiritual gifts, individual style, growth phase, and natural abilities?
4. How does your team need to refresh the job descriptions and stated responsibilities of each team member, all the while deepening your accountability to fulfilling God's determined pathway for each person?
5. Discuss with the team how each member falls into one of three categories: *wonderful, wandering,* or *wondering.* Are these evidenced on your team today and how can you draw all team members into the *wonderful* category?

5

Healthy Teams Assimilate

The names Doug and Judy Hall have become synonymous with cross-denominational, multiethnic ministry in Boston. When they first arrived in 1964, Doug was a seminary student at Gordon Divinity School, now Gordon-Conwell Theological Seminary. Their initial goal was to prepare for missionary service in India, but in the meantime, they wanted to serve "in a job no one else wanted." This led them to the "superintendent" leadership role at the Emmanuel Gospel Center where they have served ever since.

Emmanuel Gospel Center (EGC) began in the early twentieth century as a neighborhood mission in Boston. Called the "Little Church on Wheels"—a small church built on a truck chassis that served as a prop and sound stage—EGC brought the gospel message to the Boston Common. In the 1920s and '30s, thousands gathered to hear preaching on the Common from the Little Church on Wheels. Eventually the EGC moved their operation indoors and for the next forty years provided ministry to Boston's south end, mostly offering church services nightly, along with Sunday school outreach to the children in the neighborhood.

When the Halls arrived, they continued to provide these services, and subsequently expanded the ministry of EGC to evangelistic films, cooperative outdoor worship, and other neighborhood outreaches. A fundamental philosophical change transpired under their leadership, however. In the past, EGC had provided ministry almost exclusively *for* the south end neighborhood. However, the Halls didn't want to have church *for* the poor, they wanted to have church *with* the poor. And from the late 1960s until today, the expanding work of EGC has seen a significant transformation from the primarily direct, one-on-one ministry of the past to the current ministry of strengthening and supporting the work of many urban churches. This shift was the key to their present success.

The impact of the Emmanuel Gospel Center is phenomenal. The Halls have rallied a citywide team around them and have seen their own staff team grow to thirty-five members. The staff is assimilated with one another and within the community and is united around a common mission "to understand and help nurture the vitality of the church in the context of the broader urban community, particularly in Boston's low-income and immigrant communities where the work of the church is so critical."[1] They have taken the time to get to know the city, its churches, and its people. Then they have prayerfully and systematically developed, in collaboration with those most affected, appropriate programs in response to what they have learned by listening and being involved in the life of the city.

To be effective long-term, all of the programs of the EGC stress the importance of relationships and are designed with high standards. Their ministries include applied research and consulting, a citywide higher education resource center, a church planting collaborative, media and technology ministries, homeless outreach, urban youth ministry, Haitian ministries, a multicultural council that works with more than sixteen immigrant communities of the city, and urban ministry training and development. Their guiding principles tell the story of their journey and the value of their shared experiences:

- We seek the Lord's *leading and timing* in making ministry decisions.
- We seek to build *relationships* with those to whom and with whom we minister.
- We seek to build the *kingdom* of God in Boston, not just an individual, group, church or ministry (including our own).
- We seek *long-term* results.[2]

EGC works collaboratively with many different churches, denominations, and organizations in an effort to build the kingdom of God in Boston and around the globe. Their partners include local ministries, such as Gordon College, the Black Ministerial Alliance, Boston's TenPoint Coalition, the Center for Urban Ministerial Education, and the Christian Economic Coalition. And they have served several international ministries, such as the Kolhapur Church Council in India, Ministerios Urbanos en Accion, and the Oxford Centre for Mission Studies in England.

As a team that is assimilated with one another and within the community they serve, the Halls and the staff of EGC have created a model for others to emulate. They embody the principle of assimilation with excellence and are to be commended for their faithfulness to this important operating priority of team ministry. They have successfully rallied an ever-expanding team around operating principles, ministry priorities, and missional intentionality that has made a significant difference in Boston, the greater Boston region, other cities in America, and other parts of the world. To God be the glory, and to the Halls we offer hearty thanks!

Why Assimilation?

The dictionary definition of *assimilation* includes connections with physiology (to consume and incorporate nutrients into the body), linguistics (to alter a sound by assimilation; by which a sound becomes similar to an adjacent sound), anthropology (to absorb immigrants or a culturally distinct group into the prevailing culture; absorbing one cultural group into harmony with another), knowledge (to incorporate and absorb into the mind; assimilate new ideas into an existing cognitive structure), and environment (to make similar; cause to resemble). We also see this principle in the Bible. God makes it his priority to form and fashion a people around the understanding and fulfillment of a commonly shared mission, *assimilating* them into the body of Christ, where each part serves with, for, and beside the other as one. Even Webster's 1913 dictionary gives the illustration of *assimilation* as "to aspire to an assimilation with God."

God's call on our lives as believers is to be interdependently interwoven in a spirit of unity and collaboration with one another. This begins within the context of our immediate ministry teams and expands outward to the entire body of Christ worldwide. Often, however, we forget that there is a larger world of Christians "out there," and we tend to become too provincial in our outlook. That was never God's priority, for throughout biblical and church history the Lord has sought to draw his people together and unite them around commonly held and inherently shared priorities for life and ministry. It's been that way since the dawn of time and will remain so until he comes again in all his awe and splendor.

In the meantime, while we are called to serve him on this earth, we must make a choice to follow him together, assimilated into the body of Christ as *one* team for his glory. One of the best places to fulfill this mandate is within the context of our own ministry teams. It's here that the joys and challenges of assimilation are lived out. It's here that the biblical call to unity and oneness is practiced most effectively. It's here that we learn how to transfer the priority of assimilation into other current and future relationships and ministries.

Let's go back to the 1 Corinthians 12 passage. The A—assimilation—verses that describe how a healthy team functions together are 14–16 and 26:

Now the *team* is not made up of one part but of many. If the foot should say, "Because I am not a hand, I do not belong to the *team*," it would not for that reason cease to be part of the *team*. And if the ear should say, "Because I am not an eye, I do not belong to the *team*," it would not for that reason cease to be part of the *team* . . . If one part suffers, every part suffers with it; if one part is honored, every part rejoices with it.

"Here is one of the most famous pictures of the unity of the Church ever written," writes William Barclay in his commentary on the paragraph. As we have seen, the apostle Paul is drawing his picture of the church as a body, which consists of many parts but has an essential unity.

"You," Paul says, "are the body of Christ." Barclay comments:

There is a tremendous thought here. Christ is no longer in this world in the body; therefore if he wants a task done within the world he has to find [people] to do it. If he wants a child taught, he has to find a teacher to teach him; if he wants a sick person cured, he has to find a physician or surgeon to do his work; if he wants his story told, he has to find [a person] to tell it. Literally, we have to be the body of Christ, hands to do his work, feet to run upon his errands, a voice to speak for him.

> "He has no hands but our hands
> To do his work today;
> He has no feet but our feet
> To lead men in his way;
> He has no voice but our voice
> To tell men how he died;
> He has no help but our help
> To lead them to his side."

Here is the supreme glory of the Christian [person]—he is part of the body of Christ upon earth.[3]

Paul portrays the united church with the image of a healthy body, efficient in all its functions. Each part of the body fulfills its purpose, without envy or discontent toward the others.

From Paul's visual of the body of Christ, we glean the following commitments we must have to one another:

> 1. We ought to realize that *we need each other*. There can be no such thing as isolation in the Church. Far too often people in the Church become so engrossed in the bit of the work that they are doing and so convinced of its importance that they neglect or even criticize others who have chosen to do other work. If the Church is to be a *healthy body* [my emphasis], we need the work that everyone can do.
> 2. We ought to *respect each other*. In the body there is no question of relative importance. If any limb or any organ ceases to function, the whole body is thrown out of gear. It is so with the Church. All service ranks the same with God. Whenever we begin to think about our own importance in the Christian Church, the possibility of really Christian work is gone.
> 3. We ought to *sympathize with each other*. If any one part of the body is affected, all the others suffer in sympathy because they cannot help it. The Church is a whole. The person who cannot see beyond his or her own organization, the person who cannot see beyond his or her congregation, worse still, the person who cannot see beyond his or her own family circle, has not even begun to grasp the real unity of the Church."[4]

Herein lies the challenge of assimilation within the body of Christ—if we cannot see value beyond our own individual roles and relationships, we will never fully grasp the significance of unity within the body. Assimilation is a process that occurs over time as teams grow in trusting relationships and empower each other to become all that God intends for them. Assimilation is a life-giving priority of the healthy team, as it is for the healthy body of Christ.

Doug and Judy Hall and the Emmanuel Gospel Center in Boston understand this principle and live it out better than most other ministry teams. Their life together is defined by collaboration and interdependence, building associations with others that awaken the church and renew the community. They understand from the deepest places, within the fabric of their individual lives and their shared mission as a team, that God has designed us to need each other. There's nothing weak about such a need; in fact it builds strength within a team and models health and vitality to others.

But anyone who pursues assimilation and unity in a team knows that there is a price to pay for this principle to come alive. Human beings are not inclined in this direction, particularly among and within our independently minded American culture. From our earliest of days, we have been taught *not* to need others. We can live and make do on our own, thank you very much! However, if we delve deep within our hearts and souls, we will discover that we really do crave community—authentic, holistic, loving, we-need-each-other community. For we cannot live on our own, nor can we survive without one another.

Team Assimilation

Let's return once again to our definition of a healthy team:

> A Christian ministry team is a manageable group of diversely gifted people who *hold one another accountable to serve joyfully together for the glory of God* by:
>
> - sharing a common mission
> - embodying the loving message of Christ
> - accomplishing a meaningful ministry
> - anticipating transformative results

The phrase "hold one another accountable to serve joyfully together for the glory of God" articulates the principle of assimilation. The previous chapter was focused on the concept of individual empowerment; this chapter will focus on the team's serving together joyfully and for the glory of God. Serving together as a team is the ongoing work of team development, with the end result being the pleasure, delight, and glory of God.

All healthy ministry teams become assimilated into one another's lives and incorporated into a shared mission within the context of relational health. This can begin as simply as sharing one's story with other members of the team.

Patrick Lencioni describes this stage as the sharing of personal histories. In his leadership fable, *The Five Dysfunctions of a Team*, he outlines one session where the team leader, Kathryn, introduced the histories-sharing exercise. "Before we get into any heavy lifting, let's start with something I call personal histories." Kathryn explained that everyone would answer five non-intrusive personal questions having to do with their backgrounds. One by one the executives answered the questions. Hometown? Number of kids in the family? Interesting childhood hobbies? Biggest challenge growing up? First job?

Almost to a person, every set of answers contained a gem or two that few, if any, of the other executives knew. Carlos was the oldest of nine kids. Mikey studied ballet at the Juilliard School in New York. Jeff had been a batboy for the Boston Red Sox. Martin spent much of his childhood in India. JR has an identical twin brother. Jan was a military brat. During the discussion, Nick even discovered that he had played basketball in high school against the team coached by Kathryn's husband.

As for Kathryn, her staff seemed most surprised and impressed not by her military training or automotive expertise, but by the fact that she had been an All-American volleyball player in college. It was really quite amazing. After just forty-five minutes of extremely mild personal disclosure, the team seemed tighter and more at ease with each other than at any time during the past year.[5]

So often in ministry settings we have developed "functional" relationships on our teams. We tend to deal with one another from the context of how we interrelate to accomplish our stated task. By sharing our personal stories, we begin to get to know each other's joys and hurts, aspirations and fears, dreams and disappointments. The masks begin to disappear and we share our authentic selves. As a result, the team grows healthier as it becomes a group of people assimilated by love and not just a group brought together to perform a duty.

Try the histories-sharing exercise with your team. Then take time each succeeding meeting to share more—how each has come to faith, a bit about each other's family of origin, how key relationships made an impact on your life, or any other ideas you come up with that will draw your team together relationally.

When teammates know some details of each other's personal life and needs, it will directly impact the effectiveness of the ministry team. Healthy teams place a high priority on relationships, knowing that the mission will be enhanced and fulfilled with far greater effectiveness when it flows naturally from the mutual esteem of those who serve together to accomplish it. When the leader and fellow team members show an interest in the lives of one another, the team strength is increased significantly. Taking the time and effort to reinforce this principle will proportionately improve your shared life and ministry.

Assimilate through Cross-Pollination

Cross-pollination is the transfer of pollen from the anther of one flower to the stigma of another. It is also the influence or inspiration that crosses between diverse elements. For example, the American Heritage Dictionary uses the term in describing jazz: "Jazz is fundamentally the cross-pollination of individual musicians playing together and against each other in small groups" (Ralph de Toledano).

Cross-pollination occurs on teams as well. When diverse team members are united in mission and ministry, they bring to the table their respective gifts and abilities. As they are assimilated into a team, they utilize their gifts to create a new "sound," in much the same way that jazz musicians do when they make music together. In the intersection of ideas, lives, and ministry responsibilities, the team creates their "music." There's a bit of push-pull going on to produce the new sound, but after much practice, the tempo and lyrics are brought beautifully together—a wonder to behold.

When two or more people come together with an earnest desire to combine their individual efforts for the greater good, joining their hearts and hands in syncopated rhythm, the world is better served. When the body of Christ is knit together from among very diverse participants, the synergy of their collective efforts results in a new work, with new results. One goal of a healthy team is to provide a safe place for such cross-pollination of gifts. The end results of such coming together will be an increased sense of:

- accountability
- respect
- effectiveness

Team members don't work in isolation. Like the parts of a body, each needs all the others to function properly. Each member has a role to play. Each member suffers when others suffer and rejoices when others rejoice. That's the way of the healthy team; that's the way of the body of Christ.

Assimilate through Others-Orientation

When our church's recent capital campaign was launched, our pastor introduced the need for all of us to step to the plate (literally!) and pledge our support for the new initiatives outlined for our consideration. He underscored his point by bringing to our attention a box of Lego building blocks, which he had "borrowed" from his children's collection. He showed us several very ornate projects his children had recently completed—Lego houses, cars, space ships, covered wagons, and even a large yellow smiley face.

We marveled together at the myriad ways in which small and large blocks could be combined to make such masterpieces. They represented the ways God has supernaturally brought us together, and despite our color, shape, or size, made us into a masterpiece as well. At the end of the service we were all given a new piece of Lego playing blocks, with the reminder that our place on the team matters not only to God but to the people of God, the body of Christ.

The Lego display is symbolic of our need to assimilate within our teams. When we do, we bring to the team all that we have to offer. In addition, we identify ways that we feel welcomed and affirmed, brought together as a team, not singled out for solitary service. The Lego theory is that you can't create anything with one block, you need several (sometimes hundreds) to bring the team to full maturity.

In the same way, we are obligated as members of the team to consider others' needs more important than our own. The apostle Paul reminded the Philippians of this truth: "Do nothing out of selfish ambition or vain conceit, but in humility consider others better than yourselves. Each of you should look not only to your own interests, but also to the interests of others" (Phil. 2:3–4). Becoming others-oriented leads us as team members to serve other members of the team in a complementary manner, the way we would like to be served. This is the Christian way, and it's the way of the healthy Christian ministry team.

Assimilate through Systemic Direction

The next time your team meets to solve a problem, investigate a situation, or come to a decision about the future, remember the following analysis of a rather humorous case study.

> To highlight its annual picnic one year, a company rented two racing shells and challenged a rival company to a boat race. The rival company accepted. On the day of the picnic, everyone entered into the spirit of the event. Women wore colorful summer dresses and big, floppy hats. Men wore straw skimmers and white pants. Bands played and banners waved. Finally the race began.
>
> To the consternation of the host company, the rival team immediately moved to the front and was never headed. It won by eleven lengths. The management of the host company was embarrassed by its showing and promptly appointed a committee to place responsibility for the failure and make recommendations to improve the host team's chances in a rematch the following year. The committee appointed several task forces

to study various aspects of the race. They met for three months and issued a preliminary report. In essence, the report said that the rival crew had been unfair.

"They had eight people rowing and one coxswain steering and shouting out the beat," the report said. "We had one person rowing and eight coxswains." The chairman of the board thanked the committee and sent it away to study the matter further and make recommendations for the rematch. Four months later the committee came back with a recommendation: "Our guy has to row faster."[6]

Often teams analyze the situation they are in and come to a totally inaccurate conclusion. They forget that there is a systemic need or concern that must be considered. The boat race was not lost because the one guy needed to row faster. The boat race was lost because there weren't enough people rowing and too many trying to take the lead! This is obvious from an outsider's perspective, but when you're in the middle of it all, it can seem virtually impossible to find a solution.

Looking at team life from a systemic approach will aid in the ability to assimilate people, resources, and experiences into the ministry environment. Systems thinking is a wonderful way for leaders and teams to understand how their life and learning can be enhanced. Generally, systemic thought is the ability to look at circumstances holistically, seeing many different types of relationships existing between multiple elements in a complex environment. It combines our more typical way of analyzing team and ministry life methodically, systematically, linearly (A, B, C . . . 1, 2, 3) with a more synthetic or systemic approach. This is when we view our teams and ministries from a broad perspective that includes people, structures, patterns, and events all working in concert with one another. (For more information on this subject, I recommend Peter Senge's seminal book *The Fifth Discipline* and its companion, *The Fifth Discipline Fieldbook*.[7])

In many Christian ministry teams, the lack of assimilation by way of systemic thought, systemic planning, and systemic analysis is readily apparent. We tend to assess our health as a team by all the wrong benchmarks. We look more to the externals of numbers, nickels, and noses instead of how lives are being changed and systems are being created that will lead to greater effectiveness in the future. We forget that what we do affects the whole team, and what the whole team decides to do affects the individual parts. Sometimes the team makes decisions for the whole without considering the individual members or the net result of the action to be taken. Sometimes what appears to be a loss is actually a victory. Sometimes the changes that are made to the team or ministry seem devastating when in fact they are for the best.

Learning how to look at the environment of the team's life and ministry is the place to begin in becoming more systemically minded. Keep your eyes open to what's happening around you—in the wider context of your service and in the places where you are seeking to make an impact. Look at ways that your team is making a difference, in the hearts and lives of those you are serving. Pay attention to the ways your team ministry is impacting the life that's emerging in your heart, soul, mind, and strength. Be alert to perceived successes and failures that your team experiences, and don't be surprised at how God times the effectiveness of your collective efforts.

Becoming more sensitized to the systemic influences that surround you will deepen your dependence on God. He is initiating loving grace on your behalf every moment of every day—most likely in surprising, unpredictable ways—building the ministry in ways that only he can design. And he does all things with an eye toward the maturing process of his people—not in straight lines but along crooked pathways, not in controlled environments but in unexpected ways. We can't predict how he will use us or our team; therefore, it's best to remain watchful and alert to his unpredictable ways. That's what leads to a joy-filled journey!

Assimilate through Ministry Multiplication

The call of God on our lives is the simple invitation he gives to us to let him take our common lives and do uncommonly wonderful things through them. When we live in submission to his love and lordship, that's exactly what he does. And when our ministry team is inviting the presence and power of the Holy Spirit to reign over our shared endeavors, his love and lordship come shining through.

God longs for our lives to be not only in submission to his will, his Word, and his ways but multiplied in the hearts and lives of others. We don't exist on this planet for ourselves. We exist to live lives for the glory of God and, in partnership with others, to fulfill the Great Commandment (to love God with our heart, soul, mind, and strength), the Great Compassion (to love our neighbors as ourselves; to live out the Golden Rule), and the Great Commission (to make disciples of every nation, teaching others to live in obedience to Christ). If our lives are not being multiplied for his glory and grace, then we are on a team ministry path that will never produce fruit that lasts.

Assimilation without ministry multiplication is a hollow coming together of lives for selfish purposes. The result of healthy assimilation is when the parts of the team function in sync with one another and a tide of renewal sweeps in on the ministry. Only when assimilation launches us out of our comfort zones and into the lives of others will there be the blessing of God on our shared work.

When Doug and Judy Hall arrived in Boston in the mid–1960s, they found a city that was weary of independent ministry endeavors. Now, more than four decades later, the Christian community in the city of Boston is teeming with life, health, and vitality. The body of Christ is coming together in an unprecedented fashion, and the unity that has emerged from the assimilation of scores of teams is producing God-honoring results.

A Team Prayer

Loving Father, your Word is filled with challenges for your people to be assimilated as one in Jesus Christ. We embrace that truth today and ask that our team be united as one, each member needing the other. Help us today to realize that we don't walk this journey on our own; instead, we walk together in mutual love, honoring one another above ourselves. Guide our footsteps into a singular pathway that leads us to the fulfillment of your will for us. Give us joy in this journey of getting to know one another beyond our shared tasks and open up our schedules to be available to members of our team, particularly in times of personal need. Strengthen our fellowship by the presence and power of your Holy Spirit and increase our sensitivity to the directives of the Spirit. Enlighten our minds to see the holistic picture of what our team faces today, the systemic concerns all around us, and multiply our shared labors of love on your behalf. We delight to do your will, we celebrate the truth of your Word, and we lean on you for your ways to be lived out in us. Bless the work of our hands, we pray, in the strong name of Jesus our Savior. Amen.

For Reflection

1. Discuss the term *assimilation* among your team. How are the members of your team assimilated into the body of Christ, the local church, and within the team?
2. We need each other, we ought to respect each other, and we ought to sympathize with each other. In what ways is your team embodying this application of 1 Corinthians 12?
3. How are your team members' gifts being "cross-pollinated" in fulfillment of your shared mission?
4. What ways are team members showing that they are orientated toward the needs of others on the team? How are they demonstrating that they understand the systemic nature of team life?
5. Write out a prayer for your team that embraces a heartfelt desire that the work of your hands be multiplied in the lives of all you serve.

6

Healthy Teams Manage

The task ahead of him was mammoth, but we all knew he was up to it. Andrew Accardy had the skills to manage and the heart to lead, which he generously demonstrated to his fellow team members. It didn't take long for us to see that not only would our ministry take a giant step forward with him on board, but this man was destined for even greater responsibilities in the future.

Coming straight out of a Christian camping ministry in New Hampshire to the Vision New England team, Andrew had extensive experience in planning programs, overseeing staff, and managing details. When I first met Andrew, he was in his mid–twenties, single, filled with energy and new ideas, ready to take on the world. He interviewed for our conference planning position and was our obvious top choice candidate. He dived into his role feet first, and nothing was ever too big for him to tackle and ultimately handle with excellence.

Often we would meet together, strategizing how to build our annual congress to an attendance of ten thousand, a goal that was a few years off but a milestone we were fully intent on achieving. I never tired of getting together with Andrew. As a faithful team member, he was not only interested in the task at hand but always expressed interest in the people who surrounded him. He had the uncanny ability to spot good talent, and the people who were privileged to work with him spoke highly of his incredible skills and his warm heart. His sense of humor was irresistible, and he inspired all of us toward greatness, urging us to move beyond our perceived limitations and our often limited view of ourselves—objectives that were seldom spoken in our often small-minded, rather provincial New England setting.

More important, I could count on Andrew to understand the "why" of our services to churches across the region. He would frequently say, "We don't want to do an event just for the sake of doing an event." The implication of his comment was that the purpose of doing the large gathering was paramount to how we would accomplish the goal. Ask Andrew about his view of management and leadership and he would tell you, "It's not just about getting tasks done but changing attitudes and beliefs, motivating people to do something that matters in fulfillment of the larger mission." The result of effective management is the shaping of the heart and mind of the team toward the fulfillment of purpose and the leadership of people toward a much bigger calling.

Andrew came into his assignment with an explicit intention to put structure and systems into place that would function like clockwork. He reorganized files, computerized charts of complex planning, shuffled staff responsibilities, made sense out of historical records, mapped out the game plan, met with the vendors, strategized process and subsequent implementation, and ended up building a well-oiled machine. He knew that if we were ever to achieve our lofty goal of reaching the ten-thousand mark, the systems needed to be in place to support the achievement of our objectives.

Unflappable, Andrew was rarely frustrated. He took every obstacle as an exhilarating challenge to overcome. He enjoyed the opportunity to lead the team through the challenge so that no one was left behind in the learning curve. The team needed to grow through every managerial conquest so that the department was fully prepared to take the next step in their individual and collective growth. This approach worked well, and the fulfillment of the goal came earlier than we had expected.

Andrew didn't stay at Vision New England to fulfill the "forty year pledge" we made to one another (and after fourteen years, I too moved on!), but in the years we shared together I grew to appreciate deeply the friendship and partnership we enjoyed. Rick and Kay Warren recruited Andrew to join the Purpose Driven Ministry team, and after serving so well in our regional ministry, he was ready to move seamlessly into an international work of truly epic proportions. The transition into a much larger ministry was a natural next step for Andrew, having proven himself capable of all the essential tasks of ministry management.

Management Lessons

We manage things, but we lead people. This is a truism that leaders and teams must understand. We manage things: tasks, tangibles, and time, including budgets, schedules, details, checklists, facilities, databases, plans, curriculum, paperwork, resources, equipment, computers, supplies, meetings, software, structures, systems, and finances (just to name a few). We lead people. If any person is to be managed, it's you, the leader. People don't like to be managed, like an inanimate object, but they will respond to being led toward greater influence and effectiveness. Actually the goal of management is to help others self-manage, teaching them the principles and practices that will make this possible, including time management, setting priorities, stewardship of resources, and seeing tasks through to completion. When we continually do other people's jobs or watch over their shoulder as they try to do them—when we micromanage—we are thwarting their ability to learn and grow and become self-managers of their tasks and responsibilities.

Leading others is the focus of chapter 8, but the overarching principle—we lead people; we manage things—needs to be emphasized here. This is what healthy teams do. People manage things, and it's the people of the team who need to be trained in developing ways to manage the things that are before them. Without the proper management of things, the team won't be fully prepared (in fact it may be significantly hindered) to accomplish what God intends to happen in the hearts and lives of the people being served. People are God's top priority, and the transformation of lives is his daily goal. Managing with excellence will open the door and pave the way for effective ministry.

Manage with Excellence

In every ministry, both large and small, there is a lot to manage. Therefore it is incumbent on those who serve on healthy teams to learn how to *mastermind what the Master has in mind!*

In healthy, growing ministries there will always be more to manage, but it's the work of the ministry that matters most to the Master. We need to manage all of our tasks, tangibles, and time with excellence to effectively reach the people we are called to serve. Conceptually it's really rather simple; in reality it's very complex. For the team to effectively manage all of their shared responsibilities, there must be people on the team who understand the importance of management and who have the skills in management tactics that bring out the best of the team.

Common sense and follow-through are the two most important skills for effective management of team ministry.

- Common sense tells the team that there are steps to be taken and actions to be performed to get the job done.
- Follow-through reminds the team to follow up each step and action from beginning to end.

Common sense will ask and answer some very basic questions for running the ministry:

- *Who is on the team?* Leader and team members should be identified and job responsibilities outlined.

- *Whom are we seeking to serve and how will we know if we are meeting their needs?* The target group most appropriate for the program must be identified along with their needs and ways to determine if the ministry is meeting those needs.

- *What is the task?* The team must understand its specific ministry and be able to articulate it well to those they hope to serve.

- *Where and when will the ministry take place?* A facility and schedule are needed.

- *How will we pay for the ministry?* The team must work out a budget and decide if its services will be free or if a fee will be charged.

- *When do we want to start and stop this ministry?* Decide on start and stop dates.

- *How will we know we've succeeded?* An evaluation by participants and a team assessment can be used.

These are some of the commonsense management questions that healthy teams should ask themselves. Although seemingly obvious, you'd be surprised how many teams never ask them.

Follow-through issues are even more important for managing a healthy team. After the commonsense questions have been answered, there must be implementation and follow up. The execution of responsibilities in a manner befitting the task is the managerial work of the team. For example, once the team has identified the target group, they need to interview the group regarding their needs and aspirations. Taking the time to execute that work and connect with as many people as possible is time-consuming. However, planning to implement a ministry for a particular target group without first listening to them is folly.

All the commonsense questions a team needs to raise will direct the team's follow-through. Asking questions regarding finances leads to writing a budget and raising funds. Facility issues show the need for equipment, scheduling, and maintenance. Scheduling impacts the development of a calendar in cooperation with other teams potentially impacted by your planning. Evaluation evokes the need to write out an evaluation form, ask people to fill it out, and then compile the data so that lessons can be learned for the future. Each area has follow-through written all over it, and the team that learns this early on will become a healthier team.

When teams ignore the need to follow through effectively on each of the commonsense questions, the team health will diminish and their quality of service will suffer. In fact every one of the commonsense questions and answers needs to be properly executed. When one is ignored, others will be affected. It's like putting a giant jigsaw puzzle together. Each part matters if the full picture is ever to be realized.

The problem is that in the flurry of activity we begin to avoid the obvious overarching priorities and get drawn into the urgency of the immediate need. When we become more reactive to need than proactive in service, we have succumbed to the tyranny of the urgent. On an occasional basis, this is fine. In fact it's reality for all of us. But when the urgent is always supplanting the important, then the team is in trouble.

Tyranny of the Urgent

Dr. Charles Hummel, once the president of Barrington College in Barrington, Rhode Island, emphasized to his team the importance of paying attention to the tyranny of the urgent, and in fact he coined the phrase. Hummel was unrelenting in his commitment to maximizing his effectiveness in a minimum amount of time. One of the many aspects of his time management style was his recognition that without careful prioritizing and planning we will be ruled by the urgent. He knew that teams could be pulled off course and never accomplish planning for ministry that would lead them to fulfilling their most important priorities if they were continually caring for the most urgent. As he put it:

> When we stop to evaluate, we realize that our dilemma goes deeper than shortage of time; it basically is the problem of priorities. Hard work does not hurt us. We all know what it is to go full speed for long hours, totally involved in an important

task. The resulting weariness is matched by a sense of achievement and joy. Not hard work, but doubt and misgiving produce anxiety as we review a month or a year and become oppressed by the pile of unfinished tasks. We sense uneasily that we may have failed to do the important. The winds of other people's demands have driven us onto a reef of frustration.

We live in constant tension between the urgent and the important. The problem is that the important task rarely must be done today, or even this week. But the urgent task calls for instant action—endless demands, pressure, every hour and day.

The momentary appeal of these tasks seems irresistible and important, and they devour our energy. But in the light of time's perspective, their deceptive prominence fades; with a sense of loss we recall the important tasks pushed aside. We realize we've become slaves to the tyranny of the urgent.[1]

Hummel's assertion is absolutely correct. Our slavery to the tyranny of the urgent has kept us from fulfilling the really important mandates set before us. However, the key to overcoming this dilemma is first to understand what constitutes a yes for the team, and that which is a no. When a team understands their priorities and diligently seeks to maintain them, the likelihood of being pulled into the tyranny of the urgent is significantly diminished (but rarely eliminated).

Management Redefined

Once again here's our definition of a healthy team:

A Christian ministry team is a manageable group of diversely gifted people who hold one another accountable to serve joyfully together for the glory of God by:

- *sharing a common mission*
- embodying the loving message of Christ
- accomplishing a meaningful ministry
- *anticipating transformative results*

In this definition the understanding of our common mission and the anticipation of transformative results involve management. The *mission* defines who we are, what we are called to do, and how we will accomplish the task. The *results* answer the "why" of our calling—to see the lives of men, women, and children transformed by the love of Christ. Combined, the mission and results become the focus of good team management.

When the apostle Paul was writing to the church in Corinth, much of his focus was on the management of issues that had arisen in the church. His desire was to see life-transforming results multiplied in the hearts of believers and those they were serving in the city. The role of management and administration were certainly important to the apostle, but only when subservient to the overarching mission of the church.

In the book of 1 Corinthians Paul's teachings on several very specific matters of the church are filled with instructions on how to manage such concerns. His mind is sharp, his wisdom is profound, and his admonitions are poignant. Not only is he an outstanding spiritual leader, but he exemplifies a manager's mind as well. For example, after beginning with a treatise on the wisdom of the Spirit, the message of the cross, and the power of God, he reminds his hearers: "The spiritual man makes judgments about all things" (2:15). We are able to do so because "we have the mind of Christ" (v. 16) and with spiritual discernment are able to speak to issues of the day with Holy Spirit power. Therefore, it is with the mind of Christ that Paul addresses specific issues with the heart of a preacher and the mind of an administrator/manager.

On divisions in the church (chapter 3), he addresses the worldly thinking of the believers, the partisanship they are demonstrating, and the conceit they are reflecting in their boasting. He refers to himself as "an expert builder" (v. 10) who laid a foundation among them that someone else is now building on. The foundation that is built on "gold, silver, costly stones, wood, hay or straw" will be tested by fire, and the "quality of each man's work" will be tested by the flames (vv. 12–13). He recognizes that the divisions within the church are not reflective of his earlier message and he knows this must be managed before it grows out of control and destroys his intended outcome. The teaching of Paul was to be shared among the brethren so that the divisions would cease.

Paul addressed expelling from the church an immoral brother (chapter 5) and speaks directly about the sexual immorality among the believers. He reminds the community of faith that "a little yeast works through the whole batch of dough" and this kind of influence will destroy the sincerity and truth of their message (v. 6). Very specifically he tells them not to associate with a brother who "is sexually immoral or greedy, an idolater or a slanderer, a drunkard or a swindler. With such a man do not even eat" (vv. 9, 11). He makes it clear that he didn't mean the sexually immoral person of this world but those who were inside the household of faith. This kind of cleansing in the church was necessary for the message of Christ to be proclaimed unhindered in a crooked and perverse society. The specificity of his instructions offered clear pronouncements that in turn could be managed by the leaders of the church.

On lawsuits among the believers (chapter 6), Paul once again is specific in his instructions, "If any of you has a dispute with another, dare he take it before the ungodly for judgment instead of before the saints?" (v. 1). He urges the reader to suffer the injustice rather than resort to the courts. He not only speaks about lawsuits in this chapter but offers strong warnings against several other social sins: sexual immorality, male prostitution, homosexual offenders, thievery, greed, drunkenness, slander, and swindling. The overarching message from Paul is that these issues need proper management and oversight among the believers so that the message of Christ is never compromised. Manage the issues and handle them appropriately so that the ministry can be accomplished.

Paul continues throughout the book to speak to very significant issues of his day and the impact they were having on the development of the early church in Corinth (and beyond). He deals with marriage (chapter 7), food sacrificed to idols (chapter 8), the rights of an apostle (chapter 9), the Lord's Supper (chapters 10–11), propriety in worship (chapters 11 and 14), spiritual gifts (chapters 12–14), the resurrection (chapter 15), and even how to take up a weekly collection of money (chapter 16). He sums up his instructions to the believers in Corinth: "Be on your guard; stand firm in the faith; be men of courage; be strong. Do everything in love" (16:13–14).

It is appropriate to say that the apostle Paul was a leader *and* a manager. He knew the issues and concerns of the people and he led them to a deeper place in their walk with Christ. But he certainly had a handle on why the problems of his day were unfolding and he offered specific instructions for how to monitor them in a manner befitting Christ, empowered by the Spirit, and honoring to the Father. You could say that Paul had a Trinitarian managerial mind that was passionately fed by his heart to see leaders and followers exemplify the love of Christ. I can't imagine that he easily tolerated the loose ends he saw in the early church, and if he were alive today, he would be flabbergasted by the loose ends and lightweight teaching he would discover among many of our churches and ministries. He fulfilled his role with excellence and is an outstanding example for today's leaders and teams.

Manage through Strategic Plans

Knowing what the Master has in mind is the work of Holy Spirit–directed strategic planning. Listening to the Master's voice together is the work of spiritual discernment that Christian ministry teams are called to embrace. In all effective ministry planning, leaders must discern God's voice. In discernment we are able to answer as a team the basic questions: Why are we here? What is our reason for being—our mission? How does God want us to fulfill our mission?

Today many leaders do not understand the discernment process. Inadvertently we have shelved discernment, putting in its place popular techniques for decision making and planning. Instead of together relying on prayerful ways of hearing God's voice, we come into our meetings with a perfunctory prayer followed by extensive dialogue, discussion, brainstorming, and strategizing. Imagine for a moment if we were to reverse that—spending our largest blocks of time in prayer and listening together to the movement of God's Spirit in our midst, followed by team discussions of what we heard as we prayed and waited on the Lord.

Holy Spirit–directed discernment is not a new concept. Believers have been pursuing this discipline for centuries.

> The biblical concept of discernment is rooted primarily in the vision of the people of God living in a theocracy, where God guides the people in their daily lives and relationships. . . . The vision of a "kingdom of God" and a "people of God" needed spiritual leaders such as Moses and prophets to help the people come to know and experience the direct guidance of the Holy Spirit.[2]

Discernment in the Old Testament focused on the ability to distinguish between the work of a false and a true prophet. Jesus (Matt. 7:15–20) and Paul (Acts 20:28–31; 1 Thess. 5:19–22) offered teaching on discerning and testing the spirits. The Greek word *diakrisis* used here points to the capacity of a person to separate or distinguish or discern. This Holy Spirit–empowered capacity to see clearly the essence of an experience or the nature of a person or object through specific insight was the work of discernment.

Since the time of Christ, discernment has been a significant issue for the church.

> In the early church, the people of God saw their struggles as an intense conflict between God and God's forces and Satan and the demonic forces. Thus discernment was understood as the capacity to distinguish between the spirit of truth and the spirit of error, that which was of God and that which was not. . . . Paul speaks of this grace of discernment in 1 Corinthians 12 as a special gift of the Spirit given to individuals for the practical functioning, welfare, and effectiveness of the whole body of Christ.
>
> From the Middle Ages until now, Christian discernment has come to be understood as a quest, both individually and communally, for the will of God. In the context of this discipleship focus, discernment came to be understood as a process, a

method or technique by which one came to order one's life and bring all its details into harmony with God's will."[3]

Classical and modern writing and thinking on the subject of spiritual discernment have produced many helpful resources. The following is a short list of resources to consider for gaining understanding of a Christian strategic planning process with spiritual discernment at its core:

Ignatius of Loyola's *Spiritual Exercises*

Thomas à Kempis's *Imitation of Christ*

John Calvin's *Institutes of the Christian Religion*

The Wesleyan quadrilateral—the careful weighing of Scripture, reason, tradition, and experience as a discernment process

The Quaker clearness committee, with its emphasis on silence and prayer, accessing the ministry of the Holy Spirit in the context of community life

Danny Morris and Charles Olsen's *Discerning God's Will Together: A Spiritual Practice for the Church* (Upper Room, 1997) where they promote the steps of: framing, grounding, shedding, rooting, listening, exploring, improving, weighing, closing, and resting. These steps lead to a sense of peace and movement toward God's will for shared lives and ministries.

My work on discerning God's will for a church or ministry is found in *Becoming a Healthy Church Workbook* (Baker Books, 2001). I provide questions on seven aspects of ministry that need to be answered for an effective planning process to occur. All of the questions are building blocks in a church leadership team's discernment process and lead to the fulfillment of God's will for their shared life and service:

1. *Spiritual needs assessment.* What are the greatest spiritual needs of our church and our community?

2. *Strengths and weaknesses.* What are the greatest strengths and weaknesses of our church?

3. *Opportunities and barriers/threats.* What are the most significant ministry opportunities for and potential threats (or barriers) to our church, given the answers to the first two questions?

4. *Ministry options.* What appear to be the most viable options for strengthening the ministry of our church?

5. *Ministry platform.* What is the primary ministry platform on which our specific ministries should be built? This platform includes our statement of faith, vision, mission, philosophy of ministry, and listing of ministries.

6. *Ministry goals.* What goals is the Holy Spirit leading us to pursue to enhance our church's ministry?

7. *Action steps.* What action steps must we accomplish to achieve these goals?

In Lewis Carroll's classic *Alice's Adventures in Wonderland*, young Alice encounters the Cheshire Cat during her hurried attempt to find her way through a maze of a fairy-tale forest. "Would you tell me, please, which way I ought to go from here?" Alice cries. "That depends a good deal on where you want to get to," the grinning Cat answers. "I don't much care where—" a lost and flustered Alice says. "Then it doesn't matter which way you go," says the Cat, who soon thereafter vanishes—all except for the toothy grin.[4]

If you truly don't care where you are going, then encountering the strategic discernment process will be as meaningful to you as it would be to Alice in Wonderland! However, if you truly care about captivating the heart of the team for seeking the discernment of a God-glorifying vision for your church or ministry, then the steps necessary to discover that vision are worth taking. Vision inspires team members and ministry participants to focus on the hope of their collective calling; vision attracts people to fully engage in the ministry; vision builds a quality and essence of community; and vision sustains people during times when they simply need to persevere amid the trials and challenges before them.

Every ministry team needs to know what a clear vision looks like if it is to be honoring to the Lord:

- The vision must be birthed from and aligned with the Word of God.
- The vision must be consistent with the Great Commission for reaching the lost.
- The vision must be hammered out.
- The vision must be clear, concise, and easily understood by everyone.
- The vision must guide every activity.[5]

How a team discerns God's will can vary according to our traditions and styles of ministry. However, for strategic planning to occur among teams, discernment of God's voice is the top priority. Reversing our mind-set and focusing more on prayerful listening than on talkative brainstorming will lead teams to a deeper understanding of God's mission and ministry. Taking the steps that lead to that approach will significantly impact the life of any ministry team and will lead to greater health and vitality.

Manage through SMART Goals

Our God is a planning God, a strategic thinker, and he has a master plan in mind for his children. Therefore, it is right for us to pursue God's will for our individual lives and shared team experiences. Consider the following reflections of God's heart for planning, places in the Word where he makes it clear how much he delights to have his children discover his unique thumbprint for their lives and for their communities of faith. It's pure joy to know that God loves us enough to want to reveal his plans to us, and he delights to empower us by his Spirit to know and fulfill his will.

- Seek his plans with all your heart (Jer. 29:11–14).
- Seek his plans for the health of the body (Prov. 3:5–8).
- Seek his plans with the wise counsel of others (Prov. 15:22).
- Seek his plans as one in spirit and purpose (Phil. 2:1–2).
- Seek his plans to prepare God's people for service (Eph. 4:11–13).
- Seek his plans as good stewards of all that is entrusted to your care (Matt. 25:14–30, especially verse 23).
- Seek his plans so that you can know with certainty his mission (Acts 6:1–7).
- Seek his plans as you are led by the Holy Spirit (Rom. 8:14).

We need to know our "assigned task" (Mark 13:34) in the kingdom of God and then wait on him in prayerful love and obedience to reveal his specific plan to us—one prayer, one day, one season, and one year at a time. Because he wills to communicate and build an intimate relationship with his children, we can know his heart's desire for our lives and our collective experience as teams within the body of Christ.

The specifics of the Holy Spirit–empowered plan are encompassed in Holy Spirit–directed SMART goals. These are goals that the team sets together, having heard from God through the discernment process and being fully aware of the direction he is leading them to pursue. Clarifying this direction on paper and determining the focus will assist the team in discerning God's will. It's one thing to pray and talk about these matters and another thing altogether to begin to articulate the plans in terms that make sense to all.

Why set goals in the first place? Because when you don't set goals, you end up focusing your energies on problem solving. Continually gathering the team to solve problems distracts them from fulfilling their mission. Setting goals has many benefits.

- Goals concentrate our energy and attention.
- Goals move us toward specific accomplishments.

- Goals inspire greater effort than they require for attaining.
- Goals provide a basis for periodic evaluation.
- Goals bring discipline into our life together.
- Goals encourage consistency and stability.

SMART goals are the qualitative and quantitative objectives that you believe God wants you to accomplish together. They are the concrete ways you will measure ministry effectiveness and monitor your planning process in fulfillment of your overall ministry strategy. The SMART acronym identifies the qualities that goals must possess.[6] Goals must be:

- Specific
- Measurable
- Achievable
- Results-oriented
- Time-dated (to be completed at a stated time)

Leaders and teams that develop the discipline of discernment and planning will embrace the activity of articulating goals. One naturally leads to the other in the context of developing healthy ministry teams who care about the quality of their ministry management. After writing ministry goals, the team must hone them in light of the SMART characteristics above. Evaluating each goal with this measuring stick will clarify the direction of the team and lead all who are involved in the team's ministry toward a definable and transformative outcome.

Manage through Systematic Administration

Effective team management includes an ongoing care for details. Systematic administration is defined by how well the details of ministry are handled. On every healthy team, there is at least one person who has the gift of administration or knows how to recruit someone to handle this important aspect of team life.

Having led or served on a host of ministry teams for nearly thirty years, I have come to appreciate deeply the person with the gift of administration. It's important for leaders and teams to have a bright and promising vision, articulate a fabulously exciting mission, invite gifted people to serve at every level of the ministry, and set the stage for communicating the life-transforming message of Christ. But if the details of the ministry are neglected, the team's efforts come to a grinding halt.

Every healthy ministry team needs at least one person to oversee its administrative needs. Someone having an eye focused on details is essential to the fulfillment of mission and ministry. Top-quality administration is the backbone of the body, providing strength and a leverage of all available resources. When a team consciously and conscientiously cares for myriad details behind the scenes, those on the outside see a seamless coming together of all resources for shared team ministry.

Andrew Accardy knew that details mattered. He was meticulous in ensuring that people on the team covered every detail. They in turn could manage their particular responsibilities because they understood the direction and needs of the entire team. Consider managers who administrate large crusades, monitor the budget of a growing parachurch ministry, serve as superintendent of a Sunday school, or oversee a missions trip. *They all must manage well* or their ministry will collapse. *Every team* must pay attention to this need and ensure that good administration is a ministry priority.

Manage through Specific Results Evaluation

Ongoing evaluation is a required skill and discipline of healthy teams, their leaders, and all who manage particular parts of the ministry. Learning how to ask the right questions about yourself, your team, and your shared ministry leads to greater effectiveness.

Patrick Lencioni reminds us of the reasons it is important to focus our attention as teams on our collective results. He says:

> A team that focuses on collective results minimizes individualistic behavior; enjoys success and suffers failure acutely; benefits from individuals who subjugate their own goals/interests for the good of the team; and avoids distractions. Teams that are willing to commit to specific results are more likely to work with a passionate desire to achieve those results. Teams that say, "We'll do our best," are subtly, if not purposefully, preparing themselves for failure.[7]

When you make a commitment to the regular evaluation and assessment process of team life, you are making a statement about leadership development for the leader and the team. Each day you are making judgment calls on your team's ministry effectiveness, whether purposefully or inadvertently. These judgment calls focus on areas of vision, mission, commitment, competencies, building community, and changing lives. The evaluation process is a link to greater health as a team, as you continuously reshape, refocus, and renew your structures and ministries.

Creating simple evaluation tools that assess the vitality of your team or your ministry will help you see where you are strong and where you need to improve. Asking specific and open-ended questions of one another, and of those you serve, will deepen your relationships and enhance the quality of your services. Keeping the evaluations simple and asking for feedback often will create an environment for ongoing refinement and renewal.

A leader and team that are open to evaluation make a strong statement to those they serve. They are expressing an openness to learn, grow, change, and monitor progress and are showing others that no team or ministry is ever "complete" in its intention or execution. When teams do self-evaluations, they embody the transformational process of growth and maturity. In essence they are modeling what it means to be a teachable disciple of Jesus Christ, as well as a discerning team that desires more than anything else to be in the exact epicenter of God's will.

Healthy teams that learn how to manage their shared life and ministry are a wonder to behold and a delight to experience. May you and your team aspire to meet this challenge and become fully devoted to the task of Spirit-empowered discernment, strategic planning, goal setting, ministry execution, and ongoing evaluation. Remain on the upswing of the learning curve and your joy in serving together will increase exponentially and for God's glory.

A Team Prayer

Lord, you promise to be faithful to those who seek your face and discern your will to accomplish the mission you have outlined for all of your children. We claim that promise together as a team and we long to be drawn into a deeper fellowship with your Holy Spirit so that we can hear your voice and understand your call to a deeper and sweeter surrender. We open up our hearts, minds, hands, and eyes in full assurance that you will reveal your love, grace, mercy, and direction. As we strive for nothing more than you, we know that you will indeed meet us at our point of need today. You will love us as only you can. You will reveal yourself in your Word, in prayer, in silence, in creation, in community, and yes, even in the life of our ministry team. So come, Lord Jesus, and be our team leader today—enlighten our hearts and minds, give us the abilities we need to manage well the ministry you have entrusted to our care, and take us by the hand into new areas of service that will stretch our abilities and solidify our trust in you. We desire together to become a healthy team that embraces our management challenges, wanting to mastermind what you, our Master, have in mind for us. We are your servants. Lead us as your people in ways that only you can. Out of love and gratitude we pray in the name of Jesus. Amen.

For Reflection

1. We manage things; we lead people. In what ways do you need to grow in self-management?

2. How does your team need to grow in the basic areas of commonsense thinking and follow-through to become better managers of your ministry? Where does your team need to grow in becoming more attune to the administrative needs of your ministry, particularly as they help to fulfill the anticipated results of your shared labors of love?

3. In what ways does your team need to grow in their individual and collective experiences of spiritual discernment? How can you make prayerful discernment practices more a part of your team meetings?

4. What does your ministry team need to learn in order to function from a strategic plan? How do you define your vision and mission and in what areas do you need to refocus your efforts as a team?

5. Write out the three top SMART goals you and your team are attempting to pursue in the year ahead. Be sure that your goals are specific, measurable, achievable, results-oriented, and time-dated.

7

Healthy Teams Serve

On January 24, 2001, two missionaries in northwest Uganda saw their life of service nearly come to an end. They were startled by pounding on the door of their twenty-by-fifteen-foot mud-walled, tin-roofed house. A band of men were breaking down the door to attack and rob the missionaries. The two young men held them off for a while, but when the bandits started to shoot their way into the house, Reid took a bullet in his right shoulder and Erik was shot below his right elbow. The bandits beat them, robbed them, and left, assuming their victims would die of their wounds.

Immediately, Reid crawled to the CB radio that kept them in twenty-four-hour contact with missionaries located three hours away. Someone heard Reid's calls for help and began the lengthy trek to the wounded men. Around midnight their missionary friends discovered Reid and Erik. They strapped the two men into vehicles and drove them to a small hospital more than four hours away, where they received pain medication. Then they were airlifted to a hospital in Nairobi, Kenya, where, twenty-five hours after leaving their mud-walled house, they were finally able to undergo surgery and begin the healing process.

The doctors were concerned that Erik would lose his arm because the makeshift tourniquet that he and Reid had tied for him hours earlier had been on too long. By God's grace, Erik did not lose his arm and has almost fully recovered its use. Reid was not able to have his wounded shoulder repaired because of the extensive damage he suffered, so it is now fused together, leaving him with a full range of motion in his hand and elbow but not in his shoulder. Although living with a great deal of pain, Reid thanks God daily for the gift of his life.

Missionaries with Africa Inland Mission, Reid and April Satterfield responded to God's call to serve the Aringa people in Uganda. Since 1999 they had enjoyed their dream of service among this unreached tribe of African bush people, who were dominated by the traditionally Muslim influence in that part of the country. Their home church had developed a heart to support this people group, and the Satterfields captured that passion and were sent off to serve on behalf of the church. Three days before the attack by bandits, April and their newborn daughter, Emma Jane, had left Uganda for the States because grandparents were eager to meet their new granddaughter. On that same day, Erik arrived to prepare a home for his wife, Holly, and daughter, Anna, so that they could team up with the Satterfields in their mission work. Little did he know how short-lived and how dramatic that stint would be!

It is inspirational to hear Reid recount the story and the lessons his family has learned about God's faithfulness. Every moment since the time he was shot by the bandits, he has known that God is sovereign and that everything has transpired according to God's perfect plan. God's love has been powerfully demonstrated in, through, and around him and his family, and the richness of his testimony births hope in the hearts of all who hear his story.

The drama of the ordeal had a profound influence on the Aringa people. They were deeply disturbed by what had happened to Erik and Reid. On the day after the shootings, many people went by their empty, bloody house and mourned what had taken place the night before. The Muslim Imams proclaimed a fast and determined that the men who had harmed their "sons" had to be found. The people even petitioned their government to build an airfield in their part of the country so that any future tragedy could be handled in a more expeditious manner. AIM and Samaritan's Purse came alongside the local government leaders and helped them secure government funding for the construction of the airfield. When Reid and April returned a year later to visit the Aringa people, they discovered that the new airfield had been named the Reid and Erik Airfield, in honor of the men who had sacrificed while serving God and the local people. This is astonishing, considering the strong Muslim influence in the region and the fact that it was a Muslim leader's idea.

Unfortunately this story has another sad chapter. When the Satterfields left the Aringa people to pursue a seminary degree, AIM missionaries Warren and Donna Pett replaced them. The Petts were there to teach the Aringa people the skills necessary to find employment and support their families. Warren taught agriculture and Bible courses, and Donna taught cooking and tailoring. Three years after Reid and Eric were shot, seven armed men raided the small college in northwest Uganda where the Petts taught, and they killed the missionaries.

AIM's U.S. director wrote the following words to the AIM family of supporters and workers:

> The hurt of this wound is deep and too overwhelming for words. In the midst of this tragedy, I am reminded of a phrase in a popular worship song: "Light of the world, you stepped down into darkness, open my eyes, let me see." My prayer is that each person affected by this painful event will see God stepping into his or her darkness and pain. May we see and experience his healing, his perspective, his purpose and his mighty hand at work. May his kingdom come, may his will be done on earth as it is in heaven.

It's amazing that AIM plans to continue sending missionaries to the Aringa people. Their collective call to serve outweighs the tragic sacrifices their missionary team has made. Their faithful and loving service is a testimony to all of us who come alongside them in the body of Christ to serve others worldwide.

While we all aren't called to serve on the international mission field, we have mission fields among our families, neighborhoods, communities, urban centers, and workplaces where we find ourselves daily. As a ministry team functions together in reaching out to their particular sphere of influence (whether in a local church, as an outreach of a local church, or in concert with a parachurch ministry), their life as a team is defined by that service. Healthy teams serve!

The Most Excellent Way

It has been my joyous delight to have the privilege of serving on the same team as Reid and April Satterfield in our work of spiritual formation with seminary students at Gordon-Conwell Theological Seminary. Reid joined our team as a seasoned veteran in service to our great God and King. He served a people in need of the Savior, despite the challenge and without any promise of reward in numbers, nickels, or noses (the most common motivations for service by ministry teams). In fact, looking back on the years Reid spent serving the Aringa people, he can't identify a single convert to Christianity.

Healthy teams serve others not merely for the *fruit* of our labors of love on their behalf but primarily because of our willingness to lay down our lives for others—whatever it takes to reach out in love. God will bring along any increase as he sees fit. Our role is merely to serve others in his name.

John Piper defines this love and the feelings that should accompany the outward acts of love:

Love is the overflow and expansion of joy in God, which gladly meets the needs of others. Love is not merely the passive overflow, but the aggressive extension and expansion and completion of joy in God, reaching even to the poor in Jerusalem. That is why a person can give his body to be burned and not have love (1 Cor. 13:3). Love is the overflow and expansion of joy *in God!* It is not duty for duty's sake, or right for right's sake. It is not a resolute abandoning of one's own good with a view solely to the good of the other person. It is first a deeply satisfying experience of extending this joy in God to another person.[1]

Piper continues to enhance his definition of love by reminding his readers that the very nature of our longing for the abundant life of love in Christ is measured in the amount of comfort we are willing to give up to get it. The gift of eternal life is actually magnified as we are willing to hate our lives in this world to lay hold of it (John 12:25). This defines a God-centered self-denial and obedience to the call of God on our lives as his servants.

This is why so many missionaries have said, after lives of great sacrifice, "I never made a sacrifice." On December 4, 1857, David Livingstone, the great pioneer missionary to Africa, made a stirring appeal to the students of Cambridge University, showing that he had learned through years of experience what Jesus was trying to teach Peter (Mark 8:34–35; 10:29–30):

People talk of the sacrifice I have made in spending so much of my life in Africa. . . . Away with the word in such a view, and with such a thought! It is emphatically no sacrifice. Say rather it is a privilege. Anxiety, sickness, suffering, or danger, now and then, with a foregoing of the common conveniences and charities of this life, may make us pause, and cause the spirit to water, and the soul to sink; but let this only be for a moment. All these are nothing when compared with the glory which shall be revealed in and for us [Rom. 8:18]. I never made a sacrifice.

It is simply amazing how consistent are the testimonies of missionaries who have suffered for the gospel. Virtually all of them bear witness to the abundant joy and overriding compensations. Mission is the automatic outflow and overflow of love for Christ. We delight to enlarge our joy in Him by extending it to others.[2]

What is the motivation of healthy teams in service to others? Love—the most excellent reason of all!

A Healthy Team Loves

It is no accident that chapter 13 follows chapter 12 in the book of 1 Corinthians. On the heels of the apostle Paul's fabulous dissertation on the body of Christ, expressed through the appropriate utilization of one's spiritual gifts, he moves boldly into the preeminence of love. We possess these gifts from the Spirit himself, but if any of them are unaccompanied by love, they are deemed useless in the eyes of God. The primary motivation for serving in, through, and with the body—and in the context of a healthy ministry team—is genuine *love*.

The transition between chapters is: "And now I will show you the most excellent way." Paul is introducing the subject of love. In verses 4–8a of chapter 13, he lists sixteen characteristics of Christian love. Eight spell out what love is and eight say what love is not. On the positive side:

- Love is patient.
- Love is kind.
- Love rejoices with the truth.
- Love always protects.
- Love always trusts.
- Love always hopes.
- Love always perseveres.
- Love is permanent. It never ends.

On the flip side:

- Love does not envy.
- Love does not boast.
- Love is not proud.
- Love is not rude.

- Love is not self-seeking.
- Love is not easily angered.
- Love does not keep a record of wrongs.
- Love does not delight in evil.

Paul's definition of love is so straightforward that anyone can understand it. Although we tend to read this passage most often in the context of marriage, it really belongs more centrally in the life of the body of Christ. It is instruction for the entire body not simply for those who are becoming husband and wife (albeit very fitting for that occasion as well).

In the context of a ministry team, the passage could be read as follows: Teams are patient; teams are kind. Teams do not envy; teams do not boast; teams are not proud. Teams are not rude; teams are not self-seeking; teams are not easily angered; teams keep no record of wrongs. Teams do not delight in evil but rejoice with the truth. Teams always protect; teams always trust; teams always hope; teams always persevere. Teams never fail.

Imagine serving on such a team!

In Dietrich Bonhoeffer's classic text on spiritual community and fellowship, *Life Together*, he contrasts the difference between human and spiritual love.

> Human love lives by uncontrolled and uncontrollable dark desires; spiritual love lives in the clear light of service ordered by the truth. Human love produces human subjection, dependence, constraint; spiritual love creates freedom of the brethren under the Word. Human love breeds hothouse flowers; spiritual love creates the fruits that grow healthily in accord with God's good will in the rain and storm and sunshine of God's outdoors. Life together under the Word will remain sound and healthy only where it understands itself as being a part of the one, holy, catholic, Christian Church, where it shares actively and passively in the sufferings and struggles and promise of the whole Church.[3]

Bonhoeffer devotes an entire chapter to describing how such spiritual love can be fulfilled in the fellowship of the body of

Christ. His depiction of love is complementary to Paul's image of love and it is fleshed out in ways that team members today can embrace. He is fully cognizant of the challenges that communities of faith must address for love to be central to their life together. Every ministry team in pursuit of health and vitality must also address these challenges.

For Dietrich Bonhoeffer true ministry is known by the grace and service given and received among the team. Its hallmarks are as follows.

- *Ministry of holding one's tongue.* Often we combat our evil thoughts most effectively if we absolutely refuse to allow them to be expressed in words.
- *Ministry of meekness.* He who would learn to serve must first learn to think little of himself. "To have no opinion of ourselves, and to think always well and highly of others is great wisdom and perfection" (Thomas à Kempis).
- *Ministry of listening.* Just as love for God begins with listening to his Word, so the beginning of love for the brethren is learning to listen to them. Because of God's love for us, he not only gives us his Word but lends us his ear. So it is his work that we do for our brother and sister when we learn to listen to him.
- *Ministry of helpfulness.* Initially this means simple assistance in trifling, external matters. We must be ready for God to cross our path and cancel our plans as he sends us people with claims and petitions.
- *Ministry of bearing.* We must bear the burden of others; we must suffer and endure others. It is only when he or she is a burden that another person is really our brother or sister and not merely an object to be manipulated.
- *Ministry of proclaiming.* This is concerning the free communication of the Word from person to person, in which one person bears witness in human words to another person, speaking the whole consolation, admonition, kindness, and severity of God.

- *Ministry of authority.* Genuine spiritual authority is to be found only where the ministry of hearing, helping, bearing, and proclaiming is carried out. The question of trusting authority is determined by the faithfulness with which one serves Christ, never by the extraordinary talents that one possesses.[4]

Teams that choose to become healthy must choose to become more loving. Ministry teams that long for God's blessing live and serve together in the richness of God's abundant and sacrificial love. Teams that hear the call of God to fulfill such a life together will inherit his blessing. Teams that are in the early days of life together are like a child, they talk like a child, think like a child, reason like a child (1 Cor. 13:11). But as they mature in Christ together and express tangibly and intangibly the love of Christ in their service to others, they put childish ways behind them and live in the preeminence of love. In a ministry team's context of service, there is no more excellent way.

If we return to our definition, we see that love is at the heart of a healthy team. A team embodies the loving message of Christ and accomplishes a meaningful ministry to others.

> A Christian ministry team is a manageable group of diversely gifted people who hold one another accountable to serve joyfully together for the glory of God by:
>
> - sharing a common mission
> - *embodying the loving message of Christ*
> - *accomplishing a meaningful ministry*
> - anticipating transformative results

Our motivation for service is love. The healthy team not only embraces the loving message of Christ but also finds its fulfillment in the accomplishment of meaningful service to others. Teams don't exist for themselves and the joy they encounter as they serve side by side. They are called to embody the truth and life of Christ in the midst of a needy and hurting world.

Serve through Prayer

In our ministry to others on the team and among those the team is called to serve, the primary resource for every member is heartfelt prayer. Prayer is the starting point of effective service. We see this evidenced in the lives of Jesus, his disciples, the early church, the apostle Paul, and scores of other faithful men and women.

When Reid and April Satterfield entered their season of service among the Aringa people, they did so after heartfelt prayer. Their home church sent them out as representatives of the community of faith and would support them in prayer and with finances. They joined the AIM team and were called to create a team when they arrived on the field. Without prayer as their bedrock foundation, they would not have experienced the joy of serving the Lord in a distant land (despite the heartaches and suffering that would come their way). If you talk with them today, you hear a resounding chorus of thankfulness that comes directly from hearts fixed on Jesus, faithful to the discipline of prayer.

In the work that Leadership Transformations does with leaders and teams in local church and parachurch ministry settings, prayer is the first and foremost issue to be addressed. The identifier of health among any ministry team is the time they devote to prayer—private prayer on a daily basis and corporate team prayer whenever they gather together to build relationships, plan ministry, and fulfill service to others. The team that prays together accomplishes ministry together.

During one season of service with a team I led, it was a challenge to get the team to devote time to prayer. The agenda was too long or the needs were too great or the members were too distracted or the mission was too undefined. We had many excuses for not praying, and it was justified in our hearts and minds because we needed to discuss the *urgent* issues before us. *God would understand* was the unstated excuse. We allowed the pressing needs to outweigh the most important task. As a result, the fruit of our labor without much prayer was less than admirable.

When a team determines to make prayer their number one agenda item, the team thrives. Heartfelt prayer is not a perfunctory effort. It's not an opening two-minute prayer. When prayer is heartfelt, it engages every member fully, expresses the team's absolute dependence on God, and lasts for the length of time necessary to talk to the Lord and wait on him. Teams that spend large blocks of time in prayer, both in their regular meetings and ministry settings as well as on retreat together, are the teams that God delights to bless. This is not prayer legalism. Freedom and joy and excitement and delight come to teams that hold time with the Father as a precious priority. We pray at length out of our loving relationship with God and long to deepen our bond with him through lots of time together in prayer. When the healthy team prays, they are able to serve others from the heart.

Serve through Discernment of Need

When Leadership Transformations was born, a respected leader in our region, after looking at our ministry plan for the future, said to me, "What does discernment have to do with leadership development? If I were you, I'd take that word out of your documents, since most don't understand its meaning."

Too many leaders today do not understand the significance of spiritual discernment (thus the focus on discernment in the context of planning discussed in the previous chapter). And yet it's the basis for any healthy ministry team. Discernment is the process of discovering God's stated intentions for our lives and ministries. We must expend the effort to know with ever-deepening conviction the call and will of the Father. Team leadership must discern the needs of those being served as well as the direction the Lord is leading to meet their needs. Knowing how best to serve others is our focus here. Attentiveness to needs, combined with prayerful discernment, will lead teams into the embodiment of Christ-honoring service.

Retired Methodist bishop Rueben P. Job has written a primary resource for understanding spiritual discernment in modern ministry contexts. His materials have been used of God in phenomenal ways to help leaders and ministry teams get an accurate handle on the issues surrounding discernment, prayer, and service. This is what Rueben Job says in one of his prayer-focused texts on this significant topic:

> We live in a broken world. Even a casual survey of last week's headlines is enough to convince us of the fractured nature of our human family. The pain that many of our sisters and brothers bear seems almost unbearable. We want to reach out and help, but the need is so enormous that we find it easier to shut out the cries for help that come from every point of the compass, lest we ourselves be overcome with the burden of it all.
>
> We don't need to look to the other side of the world or country or even the other side of our town to find signs of brokenness. Careful self-examination reveals the fractures deep in our own lives. These wounds, old and new, also cry out for healing.
>
> The cries of the broken world are all around us and within us. How can these cries be heard as the voice of God? How can the world's brokenness be a sign of God's vision for a new heaven and a new earth?
>
> Those who have gone before us along the pathway of discernment, seeking only God's will and way, remind us that dissatisfaction with things as they are is one essential element in discovering God's will. When we are settled and very comfortable, it is hard to listen for and respond to God's voice calling us to move out, over, up, beyond, or even to new ministry where we are.
>
> The pain of our world is almost beyond our ability to bear. Because it is, we find ourselves more willing to face the possibility for radical and rapid change of things the way they are for things as they can be when God's reign is fully come. Dissatisfaction with things as they are is one of the ways that we invite the coming of God's reign in our midst.
>
> A second characteristic of those who are able to discern God's will is a passion for God's will. Along with dissatisfaction with

things as they are is the yearning for what can be. The vision of
the reign of God is not yet complete. The vision is not altogether
clear, but we believe that the One who is the truth and who
promised to give us the truth will make God's vision known to
each of us and to all of us together as we seek to listen and then
respond in faithfulness. As followers of Jesus Christ we are all
pilgrims on a journey toward God. To turn away from seeking
this shared vision is to turn away from Christ.

Another quality of the person or community that is able to
hear God's voice and to see God's vision is the capacity to remain open to God. To read the scriptures, to listen to the cries
of the world, including our own hearts, to immerse ourselves
in prayer, and to act quickly when we sense God calling us to
some simple or profound witness or service. Discerning God's
vision for a denomination, congregation, family, or solitary
life is not a simple or easy endeavor. The One who promised
never to leave us also promises to assist us, and therein is our
hope.[5]

Leaders and teams who embrace the prayerful discernment
process will discover the richness of the experience and the
joy of knowing the will of the Father. This is undoubtedly one
of the greatest of all privileges for ministry teams, who are
blessed and called out to serve the needs of others.

Serve through Fulfillment of Call

Teams that embody the principles of prayerfulness and discernment will undoubtedly fulfill the call of God on their lives.
Serving others with this certainty leads to greater effectiveness
and delight. Often the challenge for teams is to understand
and articulate their call. But when it's a process bathed in
prayer and in the context of community-based discernment,
the articulation of the call is clarified.

For example, when the steering committee of the Pierce
Center for Disciple-Building at Gordon-Conwell Theological
Seminary first began their discernment process, it was daunt-
ing to each member of the team. We approached it one step at

a time, and for several months we saw how God revealed his will and confirmed his call for the team.

The team was made up of staff, volunteers, and students. Each was consulted and engaged in the entire process. We prayed and worshiped together, listened attentively to one another, sought the mind of Christ with diligence, talked and laughed and enjoyed being together for large blocks of time, wrote drafts of proposals that included vision, mission, overview, success factors, personnel plans, policies, procedures, and goals. All the while, we stayed in close contact with one another via email, telephone, face-to-face meetings, and retreats. As a result, we were able to discern God's voice together and come up with documents that gave definition to our life in service together as a team.

This healthy team is now fully engrossed in the fulfillment of our shared call. Each person on the team understands his or her defined role, and the partnership is working well. Staff is in place, leadership is clarified, donors are delighted, volunteers have been invited to serve, and students are involved at every level of the ministry. This is a success story of teamwork at its finest, and the fruit of our shared labors of love continue to unfold.

Serve through Transformation of Lives

Bricks and mortar, dollars and cents, or numbers of people involved never solely define the bottom line in ministry. The far more important priority for healthy ministry teams is how lives are being transformed by the gospel of our Lord Jesus Christ. Is this your priority today?

When the tangible signs of ministry success—buildings, money, and people—get in the way of seeing the fruit of a life born or reborn in the Spirit, the ministry is in trouble. A healthy team will look for sightings of God at work in each member's life and in every corner of the ministry and celebrate the transformative movement of God's Spirit. Developing such eyesight among team members is an achievable goal.

The leadership team at Hope Christian Church made the choice to suspend their regular meeting discipline and focus on hearing God's voice, observing God's blessing, and identifying God's will. On a recent retreat, they devoted large blocks of time to prayer, biblical reflection, and personal sharing. This led into an in-depth discussion of how God was at work in their congregation. They began to recognize the myriad ways the Lord had been at work in their midst since the start of their church more than a decade ago.

The team at Hope was not prepared for what they discovered. Not only could they recount scores of obvious blessings, but after prayerful reflection they began to recognize many not-so-obvious ones. Life transformation had occurred at a very deep level in many individuals and the team was overwhelmed with gratitude to the Lord. The stories of these lives are still unfolding by the grace of God. The leadership team's ability to see and celebrate them has led to an ongoing priority of recognizing the transformation occurring in families, marriages, and individual lives. This will remain a priority of the team throughout their years of service.

How will your team become more alert to the ministry of the Spirit in the coming days of your shared experience? You may want to focus on the question, How have we seen God at work since we last met? in every gathering of the team. When the eyes of the heart of each member of the team are opened to the ongoing transformational work of God, the joy in serving others is significantly enhanced. Start today to look for how the Lord is moving among your team and in your ministry, and be sure to celebrate that together.

A Team Prayer

Father, we acknowledge today that your call on our lives is to become servants of others in need. We know that the heart of our ministry is to love as the apostle Paul defined it, so help us to become a team that is known more for our love than any other attribute of our health and vitality. May we truly be a team that is patient, kind, rejoicing with the truth, protective, trusting, hope-filled, persevering, and enduring in our effectiveness. May we not become envious, boastful, proud, rude, self-seeking, easily angered, keepers of records of wrongs, or delighters in any form of evil. In our childish ways, please forgive us when we fall short of your priorities for us, and lead us in putting those ways behind us. In our service to one another, may our lives be instruments of your peace. In all of our endeavors, let us sow your seeds of love in a hurting and needy world. Give us the gift of your Spirit so that we can discern your will and fulfill your call. Empower us to prioritize prayer as the vessel for deepening our loving relationship with you. Over all things, help us to keep you at the forefront of our shared efforts and to rely on your daily strength. Be pleased with our team, we pray, for the transformation of our lives and the world we've been blessed to serve in your name. For Jesus' sake. Amen.

For Reflection

1. In what ways does sacrificial love define the attitude of your ministry team today? How would you like it to be evidenced in your team in the future?
2. Discuss together Bonhoeffer's description of ministry that's embodied in the grace and service given and received among the members. How are these hallmarks apparent among your team and in what ways do you need to grow?
3. A healthy team loves. Write out a prayer that invites the Spirit to fill you with his love for your team members and those you are called to serve.
4. What are the specific needs of the people you have been called to serve? Develop a comprehensive list of those needs and ways your shared calling as a team is attempting to tangibly address those needs.
5. Celebrate together as many examples of life transformation as you can recall from your team's ministry. Praise God for the joyful privilege of serving as his vessel of love to a broken and needy world.

8

Leading Healthy Teams

Warren Schuh was the first ministry team leader I had the privilege of serving with in the mid-1970s. As a college student, I received a handwritten note from Warren inviting me to come and visit with him when I was home on spring break so that we could get to know one another. I was amazed by his willingness to meet me, a total stranger. His only connection was a letter I had previously sent to the senior pastor expressing interest in summertime service in the church. That initial meeting led to a long and meaningful relationship, beginning when we worked together on the church staff and continuing ever since as colleagues and friends.

For me, a young and inexperienced student staff worker, Warren and his wife, Connie, quickly became mentors. They were two of the easiest people to love, with gifts for pastoral work that far excelled those of their peers. As a couple, Warren and Connie were effusive in their love for one another, which taught us a lot about them. There were many times when I would stand amazed at the quality of their relationship, wanting what they had in my own marriage. Ruth and I have often commented that Warren and Connie were our number one mentors in marriage and family life. They remain in the top tier of our short list of most admired couples nearly thirty years later. Their love, laughter, transparency, and grace inspire everyone—just ask their wonderful children, who have seen firsthand the authenticity of their walk together.

When I consider role models for leading healthy ministry teams, my mind quickly leaps to Warren. He has served four healthy, growing congregations on the East and West coasts, as well as in the heartland of our country. In addition, he joined the team of Leadership Network (based in Dallas, Texas) for several years, serving the needs of pastors and church leaders from some of the largest churches in America. His peers recognize him as a man of God, filled with integrity and with gifts for team ministry. He values most his pastoral work among teams, believing wholeheartedly in the priority of people serving effectively together out of the quality of their relationships.

Warren's humility of heart is endearing to all who come in contact with him. He embodies Christ's attentiveness to the needs of others, all the while leading them to their next phase of God-directed growth and development. Not only did Warren help connect me with my first local church summer ministry opportunity, he also helped me discern the call of God on my life and invited me onto the staff team when I entered seminary. And there are scores of others to whom he ministered with encouragement, prayer, advocacy, and affirmation. I am forever indebted to Warren for his belief in and support of me and for his tireless investment in my personal, family, spiritual, and professional life.

The Church of Jesus Christ is desperate for more of what Warren embodies as a leader. The body of Christ is experiencing a massive vacuum of healthy team leaders who think more of others than they do of themselves. In many sectors of our Christian ministry world, there is a lack of such servant leadership, and it's time we consider the role of the leader in light of his or her ability to work within a healthy team. What does such a leader look like and how will we develop a new generation of team leaders?

Jesus' Heart for Leading

For today's leaders Jesus provides the most significant example of team ministry leadership. His work with his team of motley followers is by far our best instruction for our service among teams of modern-day disciples. He had a heart for leading that was reflected early in his few short years of earthly ministry.

A Beloved Heart

As he was praying at his baptism, Jesus received words of affirmation from heaven. The Holy Spirit descended on him in bodily form like a dove and a voice from heaven said, "You are my Son, whom I love; with you I am well pleased" (Luke 3:22). Jesus was beloved from the beginning of his ministry. He was beloved as a Son. He was beloved as a Savior. He was beloved in the eyes of the Father.

He boldly shared his beloved heart with his disciples and embodied this love in his servant leadership of their lives. The verbal reminder from heaven was spoken more for the observers of the baptism than for Jesus himself. His pronounced beloved status as the Son of God was confirmation to all who were witnesses of his baptism that indeed the Savior had come and the fulfillment of all previous prophecies had occurred.

Jesus is the beloved Son of God and he beckons us as his representative servant leaders to hear his words of *love*. The people of God are beloved as created ones who are adopted into the family of God by the finished work of Christ—who died, was buried, and rose from the dead so that we can know the fullness of the resurrected and abundant life. We are beloved children who are cherished and held securely in the palms of God's gentle and protective hands. We are beloved of the Father and nothing can separate us from his love.

Many ministry team leaders struggle to fully embrace the message of the unfailing love of God. Many have forgotten that we have been purchased with the price of Christ's life, death, and resurrection. We may speak about grace, but we live within a definition of righteousness that has more to do with works. We continue to strive to achieve God's unconditional love through the activity-centered, earn-his-love-through-good-works ways that dominate our ministry teams.

Warren Schuh's team leadership served as a constant reminder of how much the Father loves us. Warren expressed the heavenly Father's great love through notes of encouragement, willingness to meet with team members at the drop of a hat, his consistency of commitment to our growth in Christ, and his discipling of young leaders in their areas of giftedness. We were continually assured of the love of God in our prayers together and in the many ways he chose to love each member of the team with generosity and authenticity.

A heart for leading begins with this deeply held conviction: *I am a child of God, who is loved with a deep and unending love. The Father, who loves me as a member of his family, is well pleased with me.* The message for today's leaders is the same as it's always been—you are beloved of God. A heart for leading begins with the truth, power, and mercy encompassed in this reality.

A Broken Heart

Following his baptism, Jesus was full of the Holy Spirit and, returning from the Jordan, "was led by the Spirit in the desert, where for forty days he was tempted by the devil. He ate nothing during those days, and at the end of them he was hungry" (Luke 4:1–2). Here he is tempted by the devil to:

- Turn a stone into bread (but he refused to be focused on the bread of this world as his source of life).
- Take over the kingdoms of the world if he would only worship Satan (but he remained faithful to worshiping and serving God alone).
- Throw himself down from the highest point of the temple (but he steadfastly refused to succumb to this test or power).

Willingly Jesus entered into this forty-day period of temptation. It was not a willingness to fall into the tempting wiles of Satan but to lovingly empathize with how his disciples are tempted in similar ways. His temptations were the same then as ours are today—temptations that feed into our broken and distorted view of leadership that hungers for the feeding of our *pride*, our *possessions*, and our *power*. These were the places where Jesus was tempted—but he never sinned.

Jesus endured the earthly sacrifices of the forty days out of his amazing love for his followers as he dealt directly with the enemy of our souls, Satan himself. He was tempted but never sinned. We are tempted and we often succumb and subsequently sin.

For all team leaders today, a heart for leading requires that we openly acknowledge our *brokenness* before God. We need to come before the Father with a full understanding of our need for love, grace, mercy, and forgiveness. We must acknowledge how far we are from the example of Jesus, who was tempted but never sinned. We have and will continue to be lured into saying yes to the temptations that surround us. We have fallen into sin, and we have been sinned against. By saying yes to our temptations, we are saying no to God. That needs to be reversed. We must say no to our temptations and yes to the Father.

Are you willing to be a leader who admits brokenness? That's where you have to begin. You may recall how King David avoided admitting his brokenness. He hid his sin and continually broke one commandment after another. When Nathan the prophet confronted him, David finally broke down in absolute remorse. Psalm 51 is evidence of that sorrow, where he owns up to his sinfulness and pleads for God's mercy. "Create in me a pure heart, O God, and renew a steadfast spirit within me. Do not cast me from your presence or take your Holy Spirit from me. Restore to me the joy of your salvation and grant me a willing spirit, to sustain me" (vv. 10–12).

Some leaders are wounded by the sins of others, like Reid Satterfield, who suffered the gunshot wound of his aggressive predator. Still others are broken by less lethal assaults on their character, through verbal attack, emotional abuse, questions of integrity, or relational torment. Many suffer brokenness due to their own choices of a sinful lifestyle or choices that lead them away from God's priorities. In addition, our fears, anxieties, insecurities, and immaturity lead us into deep brokenness.

All of us have experienced a broken heart, either as passive recipients of heartache from others or by way of active sinfulness that stems, for example, from our response to inner pain, our pride, or our self-absorption. Regardless of the manner in which our brokenness is revealed, it's crucial that leaders deal with it in the context of God's love for them and invite others on the team to do the same.

It's amazing to consider Warren Schuh's track record. During his ministry tenure, he has helped countless others deal with their brokenness. In the church where we served together, he dealt with many issues of broken relationships and shattered lives. When he left us to serve in another church, he had to help that congregation heal from the pain brought on them by the sexual sin of the senior pastor. At the following church, Warren assisted the community to handle major staff transitions and the death of a beloved pastor. Only months after his arrival at his current ministry setting, the long-term senior pastor left and Warren was thrust once more into the hotbed of change, staff downsizing, budget challenges, and strategic reorganization.

Having seen the full spectrum of brokenness in those who serve in ministry, Warren is a seasoned veteran in helping leaders and teams confront their pain. There is no better way than to deal with it head-on, and people like Warren are a treasured commodity in the Christian community. You too can become that kind of team leader.

A broken heart, continuously healed by the tender mercies of God, leads to deeper assurance of how beloved we are in the eyes of God. Affirming this truth leads to a quality of team life that's driven more by humility, grace, and patience than by pride, self-confidence, and aggressive behaviors. Teams that prayerfully pursue authentic brokenness will be led into intimacy with God, healing of broken hearts, and quality of relationships with one another that will endure the tests and challenges that are sure to come their way.

A Blessed Heart

The Scriptures remind leaders that we have a blessed purpose to fulfill under the guiding hand of God. Jesus embodied the mission that the prophet Isaiah foretold centuries before his coming. In Luke 4:14–19, following the temptation account, we read of Jesus returning to Galilee in the power of the Holy Spirit. He was teaching in the synagogues when he was handed a scroll that read: "The Spirit of the Lord is on me, because he has anointed me to preach good news to the poor. He has sent me to proclaim freedom for the prisoners and recovery of sight for the blind, to release the oppressed, to proclaim the year of the Lord's favor" (vv. 18–19).

As a mission-minded leader Jesus was destined to fulfill these very words. To those present in the synagogue he revealed how *blessed* he was to preach good news, pronounce freedom, release the oppressed, and proclaim the Lord's favor. What follows in the Gospel accounts are descriptions of how this would indeed become reality. His mission was fulfilled then, as it continues to be fulfilled in our day.

For ministry team leaders, the discovery of God's mission is a joy-filled process. Regardless of the focus of the team, each member shares in the blessedness of God's intentions. Leading others into this reality is the place where God's people find their deepest longings satisfied. Leaders worthy of a following have a heart that not only desires a deep and renewed sense of blessedness but invites and encourages this attitude in other members of the team. May it be so in your team too.

By far the greatest contribution Warren Schuh made to my life is making me aware of the reality of my blessedness in the eyes of God. He affirmed my gifts and abilities, and he gently and lovingly spoke about my shortcomings and areas where I needed to grow. He treated me like a man in pursuit of God and God's purposes for my life without imposing his own intentions on me. While we served together on the same team, Warren was present in my life in intensely personal ways and he has continued to maintain contact ever since. Despite its irregularity, his ongoing presence is a gift that I treasure deeply. Because he's proven his faithfulness to our relationship, I know that if I need him, he'll be there for me no matter what. May his leadership skills be multiplied in the hearts and lives of leaders and team members in many other Christian ministry settings. The world of ministry teams is desperate for more leaders who recognize their own blessedness and affirm it in others.

Servant, Steward, and Shepherd

When we consider the life example and specific teachings of Jesus in the area of leadership, three strong images emerge: the servant, the steward, and the shepherd. Each of these paradigms corresponds with the type of leadership Jesus modeled and each is worthy of our consideration as team leaders. The three images are natural outflows of a leader who is fully aware of his or her *beloved*, *broken*, and *blessed* heart. Each provides outward manifestations of a heart that belongs to God.

Servant: Showing his disciples the "full extent of his love," Jesus kneels before them and washes their feet (John 13:1–17). He wanted his followers to understand what he was doing on their behalf and to follow his example. "Now that you know these things, you will be blessed if you do them" (v. 17). The role of a servant leader is demonstrated here and most definitively in Jesus' willingness to suffer on the cross on behalf of his followers, serving them to the very end of his earthly life. His expectation is that we will indeed do the same.

Steward: Identifying God as the master, Jesus taught many parables that reinforced the notion of stewardship in the life of the disciples. In Matthew 25:14–30 the parable of the talents brings to light this principle. When the servant-stewards are entrusted with five talents, two talents, or one talent, the Master's expectation is that each one will prove faithful in multiplying the talents for eternal purposes. Who among us doesn't long to hear the words of the Master: "Well done, good and faithful servant"? The stewardship factor in this and many other parables declares without any doubt the priority of the Christ follower to delight in caring for all that has been entrusted to him or her. Stewardship is essential to the leadership of ministry teams who are called by God to multiply every resource available to them for the glory of the Master and the expanding work of his kingdom.

Shepherd: As the Good Shepherd, Jesus came to lay down his life for his sheep. His intention was to enter our world so that his sheep "may have life, and have it to the full" (John 10:10). His desire was for his disciples to flourish under his loving care. The reality of this earnest pursuit was seen in his watchful care at the gate where the thief and robber (v. 1) would seek to enter the sheep pen "to steal and kill and destroy" the sheep (v. 10). The sheep listen for the voice of the shepherd, who calls them all by name and leads them continually to greener pasture. Each mention of the shepherd analogy has its parallel in team leadership.

The shepherd leader's number one priority is the flourishing nature of each sheep.

> For the shepherd, the reward comes in seeing that his sheep are contented, well fed, safe and *flourishing*. His energies are spent not just to make a reputation for himself, but rather to supply the sheep with the finest grazing in the lushest pasture, to store winter feed, to find clear water. Good shepherds spare no effort in providing a shelter from the storm. They constantly watch for ruthless enemies, diseases, and parasites to which sheep are so susceptible. From dawn to dusk these good shepherds selflessly dedicate their days to the welfare of their wooly followers. They do not even rest during the night; they sleep with one eye and both ears open, ready to leap and protect their own at the slightest sound of trouble.[1]

May it be so in healthy ministry teams as well.

The analogies of leadership found in the images of the shepherd, servant, and steward are remarkable. Each image (shepherd, servant, and steward) encourages the leader to prioritize the needs of the follower, who in turn grows to love and trust the leader. This kind of leader has a humble heart and a keen interest in how well each sheep is doing every step of the way. The apostle Paul tells us why we are to serve as stewards and shepherds of those on our team: "to *prepare God's people for works of service,* so that the *body of Christ may be built up* until we all reach *unity in the faith* and in the knowledge of the Son of God and *become mature,* attaining to the whole measure of the fullness of Christ" (Eph. 4:12–13).

The team leader as servant, steward, and shepherd must focus on these issues:

- preparing God's people for service
- building up the body of Christ
- reaching unity in the faith
- becoming mature in all the fullness of Christ

These are the priorities of a healthy ministry team leader. Evaluating a healthy team's leadership keeps these verses in mind: "Speaking the truth in love, we will in all things grow up into him who is the Head, that is, Christ. From him the whole body, joined and held together by every supporting ligament, grows and builds itself up in love, as each part does its work" (Eph. 4:15–16).

It's all about *them* in leadership—not about the leaders. It's more about what followers receive from their leadership than about what leaders believe they are giving to them. Flourishing leaders create flourishing followers. If leaders are becoming everything God intends for them as leaders, they will desire this in others. The empowerment of the Holy Spirit within the hearts of leaders births an intense interest in seeing empowerment emerge in the hearts and lives of the followers.

Often it's the insecure leader who has the most trouble with seeing others flourish. Secure leaders look for team members who are doing well in their ministry and show a genuine excitement about their accomplishments. It's amazing to see how much ministry can occur when leaders don't care about who gets the credit. Wayne Cordeiro offers the following checklist for a leader's self-evaluation. What kind of leader are you?

A Secure Leader	An Insecure Leader
Encourages others' attempts	Sabotages others' efforts
Points out others' strong points	Brings attention to others' faults
Overlooks flaws	Uses others' flaws as ammunition
Readily admits own mistakes	Is defensive and justifies mistakes
Gives away credit to others	Demands or manipulates credit
Rejoices when others succeed	Is jealous of others' successes
Is excited when others do it better	Is easily intimidated
Is willing to risk to improve	Plays it safe to retain position
Is content to remain anonymous	Requires others to notice
Is quick to build teams	Wants to do things himself[2]

To become a healthy team, the leader must ensure that each member flourishes in every way God intended for him or her to serve. For a shepherding leader, the instinct is to find greener pasture for the flock under his or her care. The inclination of the shepherd is to nudge the sheep in that direction, for their own good. When the shepherding leader seeks out the interests of the followers and protects them from the enemy's attacks, the spotlight is appropriately on the needs of the sheep. The measure of an effective shepherd, therefore, is whether the "sheep" are flourishing as they hear the voice of the shepherd leading them to Jesus, the Good Shepherd. With this as a benchmark, how well is your team being led?

Trinitarian Model of Leadership

In the book of 1 Corinthians the apostle Paul describes the ministry of leaders as stewards, "servants of Christ . . . entrusted with the secret things of God. Now it is required that those who have been given a trust must prove faithful" (1 Cor. 4:1–2). Later in 2 Corinthians Paul describes ministers of the new covenant by giving thanks to God:

Who always leads us in triumphal procession in Christ and through us spreads everywhere the fragrance of the knowledge of him. For we are to God the aroma of Christ among those who are being saved and those who are perishing. To the one we are the smell of death; to the other, the fragrance of life. And who is equal to such a task? Unlike so many, we do not peddle the word of God for profit. On the contrary, in Christ we speak before God with sincerity, like men sent from God.

2 Corinthians 2:14–17

The great evangelist Luis Palau, while preaching from this passage in 2 Corinthians at a conference in January 2001, reminded teams and leaders of our high calling, and our need to exude the aroma of Christ, the fragrance of life. We are to embrace and embody:

- unquenchable optimism (v. 14a)
- unwavering success (v. 14b)
- unforgettable impression (vv. 15–16)
- unimpeachable integrity (v. 17)

Dr. Palau's admonition enlarges what the apostle Paul is emphasizing as he teaches the Corinthian church about leadership. The confidence leaders are to have today is the same courageous confidence of the church in Corinth: "Such confidence as this is ours through Christ before God. Not that we are competent in ourselves to claim anything for ourselves, but our competence comes from God. He has made us competent as ministers of a new covenant" (2 Cor. 3:4–6).

God himself is the source of our ability to lead ministry teams today as ministers of the treasures of the gospel. These treasures lead to the abundance of life promised to us by God the Father, Son, and Holy Spirit. He will not abandon us after he issues to us a call to leadership. In fact not only will he remain by our side as the one who empowers us for service, but he will continually direct us as leaders and team members in the way he wants us to go. This is the promise of the Trinitar-

ian God who created, designed, called, and equipped us for a
lifetime of service.

To wrap our arms around a Trinitarian understanding of
team leadership, it's important to consider the various roles
and functions that would be necessary elements of such a con-
struct. These guiding principles have been outlined by Charles
Olsen and Ellen Morseth as unifying, loving, and interactive
priorities for team leaders to consider.

> Two biblical texts provide foundational insight to this model:
> Ephesians 1 and Colossians 1. In those texts, the Creator, first
> person of the Trinity, blesses, chooses, reveals a design, plans,
> gathers, unifies, and works within the fullness of time. So one
> function of leadership is to call forth and employ the gifts of
> those who can bless and affirm the community's story, make
> strategic choices, plan, care, and tend the life of the organization
> within an ordered framework of time.
>
> The second person of the Trinity—Servant Redeemer—serves,
> forgives, grants inheritances, reflects God's image, engages the
> creation, holds all things together, reconciles earth and heaven
> (worship and work), and is a locus of God's dwelling. A second
> function of team leadership is to provide services and resources
> that put flesh on the particular charisma of the organization.
> Servant leaders who bear the mark and mind of Christ exercise
> this integrative and reconciling role.
>
> The third person of the Trinity—the Spirit—reveals love, fills
> with wisdom, stimulates growth and fruit bearing, provides
> energy and inspiration, and seals the community in word and
> truth. So a third function of team leadership is to read the signs
> of the times, listen closely to discern the Spirit's stirring in both
> social and ecclesiastical cultures, and look for new gifts and
> callings that may be offered.[3]

Understanding and fulfilling a Trinitarian model of leadership provides a joyful way of leading the ministry teams
under our care. God's empowerment in this well-rounded
model will lead us into a deeper dependence on him as we
embrace his call as servants, stewards, and shepherds of the
flock of God.

One Leader

Every team needs a leader. Even teams of leaders need one leader. When more than one person is charged with the responsibility of leading, confusion reigns on the team. No one can serve two leaders, for if you try to do so, you are destined for disappointment, distraction, or destruction.

It's not true that everyone on a team is equal, all opinions count the same, or that a team can function without leadership. John Maxwell calls this the "myth of the roundtable. A team that tries to function like a democracy never gets anything done. The truth is that everyone on a team is important, but not everyone is equal. In the eyes of God, everyone is loved equally, but when it comes to leading the team, somebody needs to step forward."[4]

When both of my elderly parents were in their final weeks of life, we confronted the reality of their needs as we dealt directly with the medical community. Each hospital and nursing facility they were in espoused (even bragged about) their team approach to caring for their patients. However, from a patient and family perspective (and from a leadership perspective), they never embodied a healthy team approach. Instead, they were a work group with no stated leader. The doctor, who was designated as leader, was present only during rounds. The nursing team was continuously in flux, not only with daily rotations but throughout the week. The charts contained abbreviated notes about the medications and a timetable for dispensing services, but there was never enough written about circumstances that required additional care. When it was time for family meetings, each member of the team deferred to one another and we were left dissatisfied every single time. Without our hands-on advocacy on our parents' behalf, they would have been left unattended by this "team" approach many times throughout their final weeks of tenuous health.

This is not to criticize the healthcare system my parents were in but merely to point out the lack of leadership on these supposed "teams." This is merely one example of countless systems that use team language to describe their collaborative work.

But, whether it's in politics, business, families, communities, or even in churches and Christian ministries, we have a lot to learn about team leadership.

Every team needs one leader, and every team needs the right leader. It sounds rather simple, but many teams today are leaderless, double-visioned, or inappropriately led by the wrong person. It's time to reverse this curse on teams and start leading teams in healthy, intentionally focused ways.

First of all, it's important that every team have *a* leader. Jesus was the clearly defined leader among his band of disciples. They looked to him for leadership, and he provided it with excellence. In the early church, men like Peter and Paul were clearly defined leaders and the first Christian church fathers followed their lead. Throughout church history there have been many notable leaders, and the church remains intact today as a result. God loves to call and bless the work of his leaders, and each team must have a leader. Otherwise, chaos and confusion will reign.

Second, it's vital that every team have *one* leader. Two-headed, double-visioned leadership doesn't work in healthy ministry settings. Even when two or more are designated as a leadership team, set apart from the team membership, there must be a clear delineation of each person's responsibilities from the beginning. If a senior pastor and executive pastor don't have distinctly defined roles, then they may jockey for each other's position and cause confusion among the team. If a ministry executive has a senior vice president, the same admonition applies. A president or pastor and a board chairman must also work out the uniqueness of each role. Twofold leadership can work only when the definitions are clear and triangulation, or going around one leader to get to the other, is forbidden. Count the cost of a multiple leadership paradigm and plan accordingly to ward off any future troubles for the team.

It's also crucial that every team have the *right* leader. Once the leader has been determined, it's vital that he or she take the leadership position and fulfill the leadership responsibilities. If not, a more vocal or powerful member of the team will step into the leadership vacuum and inappropriately assume authority for the group. Or if weakness is perceived in the leader, members will take turns leading inadvertently (or proactively) so that some kind of leadership is provided. Whether de facto or de jure, a leader will *always* emerge in every team, but often he or she may not be the right person for the job. Right leadership for every team is an essential ingredient of health. Identify the appropriate leader for the team, and then trust, equip, and support the leader in carrying out this extremely important role.

George Barna describes the *one right leader* on the ministry team as the "captain" of the team, defining two unique roles of the captain and five ways he or she leads the team:

> How does a captain capably perform this duty of keeping the team focused, productive, and mutually supportive without derailing his or her own unique leadership contribution to the common cause? This individual must have the ability to balance two unique roles: (1) the specialization he or she provides in the leadership mix, and (2) the function of a process facilitator. To faithfully carry out this dual role, the captain juggles leadership within the ministry focus.
>
> 1. The captain maintains the team's focus on the vision.
> 2. The captain facilitates positive and productive relationships among team members.
> 3. The captain identifies opportunities for individual growth.
> 4. The captain prepares the team to move ahead by acquiring resources.
> 5. The captain demonstrates personal leadership productivity.[5]

Barna's description of the team captain's role parallels the work done by Jon Katzenbach and Douglas Smith in their best seller *The Wisdom of Teams*.[6] In this classic team-building textbook, the authors focus on what it takes to create a high-performance organization. They agree that leadership is a fundamental value of any healthy team and are convinced that leaders don't necessarily need remarkable leadership qualities or even extensive training. They simply need to *believe in their purpose and their people*. When they do, they are effective team leaders who are instinctively able to strike the right balance between action and patience as they provide good team leadership. Successful team leaders do the following:

- keep the purpose, goals, and approach relevant and meaningful
- build commitment and confidence
- strengthen the mix and level of skills of team members
- manage relationships with outsiders, including removing obstacles to team effectiveness
- create opportunities for others to perform
- do real work themselves, equivalent to that of other team members

Successful team leaders never:

- blame or allow individual team members to fail
- excuse shortfalls in team performance

You know you are on a healthy team when the leader is fully aware of your needs, gifts, and aspirations and seeks ways to place you in a context in which you can serve with excellence.

Redemptive Leadership Model

Leadership of teams is much more about community than it is about the individual. When the individual member of a team is brought into the fullness of life within the context of a healthy team, the leader and the team members thrive. In such cases the character of a leader defines the vitality of the team process.

A team leader who is aware of the reality of this leadership process—a *person* involved in a *process* of leading a group of *people* toward the fulfillment of a *purpose* under the *power* of the Holy Spirit—can be used by God to accomplish his purpose.

Let's look at the key elements of this definition of a leader.

Person. In every team there is a person who serves as the leader and that person needs to be aware of his or her personality, gift mix, and contribution to the ministry team through the fulfillment of this responsibility.

Process. The leader understands that the ministry is never completed; it will always be a work in process and therefore will need continued refinement.

People. The team functions within the flourishing nature of members of the team who are called, gifted, and empowered to serve together. A healthy team leader is aware of the learning curve of each member and leads him or her to the next most natural place of growth and development.

Purpose. The team leader ensures that each member serves side by side to accomplish a shared vision, mission, and ministry.

Power. The team leader knows that the only way to do effective ministry is through the power of the Holy Spirit as he directs the ways of the team and leads them to fulfill their shared calling in the Lord.[7]

Remember our definition of a Christ-centered team:

A Christian ministry team is a manageable group of diversely gifted people who hold one another accountable to serve joyfully together for the glory of God by:

- sharing a common mission
- embodying the loving message of Christ
- accomplishing a meaningful ministry
- anticipating transformative results

Add to this our definition of a team leader:

> A Christian ministry team leader is a *person* involved in a *process* of leading a group of *people* toward the fulfillment of a *purpose* under the *power* of the Holy Spirit.

Combining the definitions of team and team leader brings together a redemptive, transformative model of team ministry. The dynamics of team life in service to others is fulfilled when we understand the complexity of teams and the holistic practices into which teams are called. Instead of a list of characteristics that leaders check off about themselves or their team, this model becomes more living and active. In the constancy of team life, leaders must learn to be adaptive and agile. Leadership is not a static activity, for the world is ever changing and the needs of people are continually being redefined, refined, and refocused as the seasons of their lives evolve day by day, season after season.

A redemptive understanding of leadership keeps the leader's eyes wide open for opportunities to serve team members and those to whom the team is called. Holding fast to a dynamic model of vitality in team life will bring about the fulfillment of transformative traits of leaders, such as persistence, self-knowledge, a teachable spirit, emotional maturity, willingness to take risks, no fear of failure, and a strong sense of mission. When the leader is aware of these characteristics and is able to draw them as needed from his or her well of inner resourcefulness, a rich team life develops. This does not happen if the leader acts in a static, linear, or robotic fashion.

Healthy leaders of healthy teams are those who embody this basic definition of leadership and are flexible to lead others in a dynamic context of service that is never fully perfected. It's in the experience of team life, embracing the timeless truths from God's Word in the milieu of our day, where the leadership dynamic emerges. Leaders who wish to leave a lasting legacy will lead with an eye on the future.

In a redemptive and transformative model of team leadership, healthy ministry teams are led by those who are:

Called. First and foremost God has gifted and empowered the leader to serve him in this unique place of ministry.

Commissioned. The larger ministry context invites, affirms, and commissions the team leader to be responsible to lead the team.

Compassionate. The leader is aware of the needs and aspirations of each team member as well as those of the people the team has been asked to serve.

Capable. With a teachable spirit, the leader is willing to grow in areas of greatest capacity and giftedness, all the while empowering others to do the same.

Committed. The leader is tirelessly faithful to the overall vision and mission of the team, the members of the team, and all those who are being served.

When a team has a leader with these capacities evidenced in his or her personal and ministry life, the team is destined to grow into greater health and vitality. For those aspiring to such leadership, these traits become the focus of their prayers for deeper spiritual vitality and increased effectiveness in servant leadership within their team. Teams are crying out for such leadership today and the redemptive, transformative model that comes from Christ's example as servant, steward, and shepherd becomes ours as well.

Jesus asks, "Do you love me?" Jesus sends us out to be shepherds, and Jesus promises a life in which we increasingly have to stretch out our hands and be led to places where we would rather not go. He asks us to move from a concern for relevance to a life of prayer, from worries about popularity to communal and mutual ministry, and from a leadership built on power to a leadership in which we critically discern where God is leading us and our people. Be a leader with outstretched hands, who chooses a life of servanthood. It is contained in the image of the praying leader, the vulnerable leader, and the trusting leader.[8]

A Team Prayer

Lord Jesus, the call to servant leadership on a ministry team is a high call and a profound privilege. Your commission of grace and love on our team leaders is our fervent prayer. Our leaders need a fresh empowerment of your promised Holy Spirit, so today we cry out for the work of your Spirit in the midst of our ministry. Shepherd our leaders as only you can do. Breathe on them the breath of your abundant life. Fill them with gifts and abilities sufficient to the needs of our ministry. Grace them with the fruit of your Spirit—love, joy, peace, patience, kindness, goodness, faithfulness, gentleness, and self-control. May the evidence of your mercy, power, and presence be manifest in our shared ministry responsibilities today. May the work we accomplish together flourish under your gracious tutelage. We lean in your direction and entrust our leaders to you as people who are praying, vulnerable, and faithful. May our leaders acknowledge their beloved place on your breast of love, may they become fully aware of their brokenness, and may their blessedness become our blessedness as they embody your holy purposes for their lives. We look to you as our Good Shepherd and we listen intently for the sound of your gentle voice today. Speak, Lord, for your servants are here to listen for your instruction and for the leading you provide through our earthly leaders. May the work of our hands be for your glory and the building up of your kingdom, Father, Son, and Holy Spirit. Amen.

For Reflection

1. What are the traits of a healthy leader that you most appreciate? Give examples of people you admire who embody these traits.
2. Discuss ways you can be present with one another as you come to grips with your beloved, broken, and blessed status in the eyes of the Father.

3. Which image of Jesus' call to leadership—servant, steward, shepherd—are you most drawn to and why?
4. In what ways can the leader of your team be encouraged to grow as a secure leader, one who can captain well the team under his or her care?
5. How can the redemptive model of leadership be evidenced in your life and within your team in the future?

Conclusion

Becoming a Healthier Team

Joining the team at Gordon-Conwell Theological Seminary's Pierce Center for Disciple-Building has been a delightful experience since day one. It was enhanced from the beginning by my relationship with Barry Corey, academic vice president and dean at the South Hamilton, Massachusetts, campus. Consistently Barry functions in his role out of a deep and abiding sense of loyal commitment to serving the best interests of others. This is evidenced in Barry's life and ministry through his faithfulness and love, demonstrated daily to each member of the team.

Prior to my arrival, Barry was the leader of the Pierce Center team. He continues to champion the cause of the Pierce Center among the administration, faculty, steering committee, and student body. He understands the importance of the center in the life of the seminary community and is first to step to the plate on our behalf. He frees me up to direct the day-to-day efforts of the center, which is designed to foster the habits of the heart, deepen spiritual community, and train our students in discipleship. The center plays a unique role as a resource for seminarians, helping them balance the strong academics and skill development they are receiving with care for their soul.

A major part of my responsibilities among the center's team is to lead the staff and work closely with dozens of students who are advocates and ambassadors of the center on all three campuses, serving a total of more than two thousand students.

The center plays a significant role among the entire seminary community and our charge is large. Barry, the steering committee, staff, and students all came to the realization that for the center to fulfill its demanding charter, mandate, calling, and objectives, we needed to be assured of the commitment level of everyone involved in the program.

Covenants

It was the signing of a covenant that significantly enhanced our life together as a team. The promises we made to one another—seminary to students and students to seminary—are articulated in a one-page covenant that every member of the team had a role in creating. In fact all the principal parties spent the better part of six months in ongoing prayer and dialogue to create this excellent document.

After prayer, we wrote a document, discussed and edited it several times, until we finally agreed we had a covenant we could use. We distributed it to the entire team, including each of our students who were beginning the new academic year. At our fall retreat in September, we closed our time together with a covenant signing ceremony. Each student came forward one at a time and placed their signature on the bottom of the document, which was also signed by the staff from each campus. The promises we were making before God and in the presence of one another were solemn. We were pledging to serve as a team for the coming year in a variety of important ways. We all knew that there would be mutual accountability concerning these promises as the year progressed. As a result, we as a team forged a deep level of commitment.

In the covenant, we outline several significant issues:

- *The mission of the center.* For example: The Pierce Center for Disciple-Building is designed to prepare ministry leaders who prioritize intimacy with Jesus Christ and the development of effective disciple-building skills within the context of a healthy Christian community.

- *The responsibilities of the seminary to the students who receive scholarship aid from the center.* For example: As a member of the Pierce Center Fellowship, you can expect from the seminary:

  1. Tuition aid for full-time students

  2. Prayerful support and encouragement from the Pierce Center campus director through:

     One-on-one sessions with the center's campus director

     Occasional socials with students, staff, spouses, and families

  3. Training in spiritual formation and disciple-building via:

     Fall and mid-year Pierce Center retreats

     Annual disciple-building forum and special training events

  4. Disciple-building resources and preparation for post-graduate ministry experience

- *The responsibilities of the student who receives scholarship aid and participates in leading the center's activities on campus.* For example: As a member of the Pierce Center Fellowship, you commit to the work of the Pierce Center in the following ways:

  1. Involvement in small groups by:

     Facilitating a weekly or biweekly soul care small group on campus

     Participating in biweekly spiritual formation group meetings with the center's campus director and other Pierce Center Fellowship members

  2. Promote the Pierce Center activities among the campus community. This will include:

     Participating once per semester in one of the Pierce

Center ministry teams of your choice (focused on soul care small-group facilitation, spiritual formation, or disciple-building training and resource development)

Advocating for additional Pierce Center programs among the student body (Soul Sabbaths, Annual Forum on Disciple-Building, and other special events)

Writing a covenant is challenging. It requires an unbridled commitment of the leader and team members to create a statement that speaks to the specific life of the team. A covenant needs to reflect the unique traits of the ministry and the team. When written in the context of community, all concerned will embrace it with ease. If only the leader or one member of the team creates the covenant, it will not have the same impact.

The process of creating a covenant among the Vision New England staff team was very different from the way the Pierce Center accomplished it. When the Vision New England staff first wrote our covenant, we were on retreat together. We spent considerable time talking about what makes a healthy team. We prayed through a variety of Scripture passages, discussed implications for our shared ministry, and brainstormed priority issues that meant the most to our particular setting.

For an entire afternoon, we answered the question, What are the characteristics of a healthy team? We wrote our answers on sticky notes, one trait at a time. Then we grouped the notes into summary categories and defined each category. After that we spent time discussing each trait that had landed in the major categories and wrote out statements that summarized our comments. By the end of the retreat we had developed the first draft of our team covenant, which grew out of our extensive, prayerful discussions.

The major categories of our covenant fell into the areas of:

- humility
- harmony
- honor

- honesty
- hope

These categories come to life in five key paragraphs of the covenant:

As a member of the Vision New England staff team, I hereby covenant, by the grace of God, to walk with my colleagues in Christ-like humility, submitting my personal agenda to the well-being of the whole team.

With loving concern, I will encourage, affirm, and support my teammates. Forsaking covetousness, I will recognize their diverse gifts and submit myself to the unity of the Spirit which Christ commands us.

I will passionately commit myself to excellence as I seek to fulfill God's call in my life. I will persevere even when the cost for me is high. I covenant to discover and support common desires and goals that are established in our behalf as we seek to pursue a shared vision for ministry in our region. In my efforts to work harmoniously within the team, I agree to abide by commonly upheld principles and will be open to change whenever necessary in submission to our clearly stated purposes. In my connections with others who are observing our team in action, I will make every effort to assume uniformity and consistency in my message through written and verbal communication.

I will seek to view others as God sees them and will consider it a fundamental truth that not only do my teammates need me, but that I need them as well. I will strive to learn, understand, appreciate, and honor the uniqueness of others on the team. I will commit to developing and maintaining healthy relationships with my team members, realizing that our fellowship will have a positive net effect on the health of our shared ministry. I will strive to demonstrate an enthusiastic, positive attitude toward my team members. I will spend time with my team members for the purpose of fun, rest, and reflection.

By the grace of God, I will seek to respect each member of the team through honest and healthy communication. I will seek to resolve conflict by forgiving others, accepting constructive criticism, and by allowing feedback through a mutually agreed upon third party, if necessary. I will challenge my teammates in a flexible, non-threatening manner, and will submit myself to being accountable for my own actions.

I will take advantage of every opportunity to develop my skills and will seek training to increase my knowledge in areas of my responsibility and improve my personal skills. I will encourage creativity and empower those on my team to serve with excellence unto the Lord. I will seek to help provide the resources needed in order to get the job done. By fulfilling the terms of this covenant, I will foster a mutual sense of accomplishment and significance among all team members.

Signed _____ Date _____

By creating the covenant as a team, with everyone giving input to the process and to the final product, we ended up with a longer covenant than expected but one that was owned by the entire team. We spent time during subsequent staff meetings reminding each other of the covenant we had signed in each other's presence. In addition, we took time during these meetings exegeting the five key topics and paragraphs of the covenant. It was exciting to see how these topics came to life as we applied them practically to our team experiences.

Senior pastor George Cladis and the staff team at Noroton Presbyterian Church (NPC) in Darien, Connecticut, also defined their life together in the form of a covenant. It's articulated fully in Cladis's book *Leading the Team-Based Church* and is based on three primary biblical texts:

> *As a prisoner for the Lord, then, I urge you to live a life worthy of the calling you have received. Be completely humble and gentle; be patient, bearing with one another in love. Make every effort to keep the unity of the Spirit through the bond of peace. There is one body and one Spirit—just as you were called to one hope when you were called.*
>
> Ephesians 4:1–4

> *Speaking the truth in love, we will in all things grow up into him who is the Head, that is, Christ. From him the whole body,*

*joined and held together by every supporting ligament, grows
and builds itself up in love, as each part does its work.*

Ephesians 4:15–16

*Be imitators of God, therefore, as dearly loved children and
live a life of love, just as Christ loved us and gave himself up
for us as a fragrant offering and sacrifice to God.*

Ephesians 5:1–2

Here is part of the covenant:

We, the staff of NPC, desiring to be faithful to Christ in our
relationship with each other, and to model the love and unity
as demonstrated by the Father, Son, and Holy Spirit, do covenant to the following:

- Seek to appreciate and live out our God-given individual blessings with a sense of awe.
- Intentionally encourage and bless one another.
- Draw out each other's gifts while making the weaknesses irrelevant.
- Put an emphasis on self-grace and grace with one another rather than perfection.
- Speak well of fellow staff to others.
- Forgive one another and ourselves.
- Work through problems rather than bury issues.
- Disagree openly, avoiding triangulation and speaking unkindly of others.
- View all ministries as an interlinking circle; no beginning, no ending, no one more important than the other.
- Like the potter and the clay, be willing to be molded and changed.
- Communicate, both to each other and to the congregation.
- Make time for fellowship, worship and prayer together.
- Respect, honor, and trust each other.[1]

John Maxwell gives us another example of a covenant. This
one uses the simple acronym for the word *partner*. Maxwell's
thoughts on partnership grew out of one of Mother Teresa's

wonderful quotes: "You can do what I cannot do. I can do what you cannot do. Together we can do great things." Maxwell promotes partnership within his ministry at InJoy and has put this acronym to practice among his staff team. He writes:

As your partner, we promise to . . .

Put your needs first in every situation.
Add value to your personal leadership.
Recognize we serve a common goal.
Tailor our services to meet your need.
Never take for granted the trust placed in us.
Embody excellence in everything we do.
Respect everyone's uniqueness.[2]

A covenant for your ministry team will significantly enhance the quality of your shared experience. It will take time to create one that fits the milieu and purposes of your team, but it's worth every ounce of effort. There's nothing like keeping your word and fulfilling your covenant to God and one another. Don't lose sight of its importance as you struggle to design a covenant that fits you as you become a healthier team.

Retreats

Off-site gatherings of the team enhance relationships—with God and one another—and provide leverage for the work you share in common. Taking the time for retreats should become at minimum an annual tradition for a healthy ministry team. Finding the appropriate time and venue that fits the purposes and priorities of the team may be the hardest task of all. Creating an agenda for the retreat flows out of your shared experiences and feeds into the development of your team for the future.

What is the purpose of your retreat? What do you hope to accomplish on retreat? What will you actually do while on retreat? What do you envision bringing home from the retreat? What do you long to see emerge in your team as a result of the retreat? These are some of the primary questions teams must wrestle with as they begin to design the elements of a retreat.

Retreats have differing purposes. Some are used for the spiritual refreshment of the team. Others are created for long-range planning. Still others are focused on team-building exercises. Some teams use a retreat as a break from the action of life and ministry. Some seek to combine a few of these objectives. Whatever your purpose, design the elements of the retreat to accomplish it.

If you are planning a retreat for spiritual refreshment and renewal, be sure there is plenty of time allowed to listen to God. Worship becomes central to the team experience in such a climate. Time for personal sharing of team member's stories will bring the people together. Scheduled opportunities for quiet prayer and reflection will feed the soul. Relaxed time lingering at meals together or even experimenting with a silent meal will deepen the fellowship. Teaching on subjects that will move the heart of the members in deeper love and devotion to Christ is essential. To add to the value of the retreat, include reflection exercises on a few choice topics for pondering and processing. There are numerous options for designing a retreat for the spiritual refreshment of the team. Choose the best ideas for your specific group and go for it.

A retreat that focuses on strategic or long-range planning will look and feel much different. There will be some of the elements of the spiritual refreshment retreat described above, but other elements must be included. If you desire to enter into a planning cycle, be sure to allow time for prayer and seeking the heart and mind of God for your planning. It's critical that you listen to God's directives for your ministry instead of merely brainstorming the best ideas. Spiritual leaders understand that fundamentally we are called to lead and serve from the heart. Therefore, paying attention to the needs of the heart is critical to your retreat's success.

There are numerous ways to use a retreat in creating or enhancing the strategic planning of the ministry team. Determining where your team is on a basic continuum of planning is key. Are you at the starting point, nearing completion, or somewhere in between? Identify what planning questions need to be addressed and stay focused primarily on those issues. No retreat can cover every possible planning issue nor can one retreat be the sum total of a team's planning efforts.

Some of the possible planning questions your team could raise include:

1. What are the spiritual needs of the community we are seeking to serve?
2. What are our greatest strengths as a team in meeting those needs?
3. What are our greatest concerns, shortcomings, or liabilities that require attention among our team in seeking to meet those needs?
4. What are the largest opportunities before us in addressing creatively the needs of the ministry we have been called to lead or serve?
5. What obstacles or barriers are standing in the way of working toward the fulfillment of our dreams and opportunities to serve?
6. What goals can we articulate together that will define the focused priorities of our upcoming season or year of service?
7. What are the action steps to be taken and in what order should they be prioritized in the coming months?

Before the retreat comes to an end, be sure to decide who is responsible for each action step. Delineate specific roles team members will play in accomplishing these steps and decide on the time frames for them to be achieved. Be sure that everyone knows why the action is being pursued.

You may also want to evaluate your goals with the SMART acronym:

Specific. Are the goals and action steps specific?

Measurable. Are they going to be easily measured when complete?

Achievable. Are they within reach and reason for our team?
Results-oriented. Is their purpose clear?
Time-dated. Have completion times been determined?

Getting to the place where your team is ready to articulate on paper the specific desired actions will be the joy and challenge of the retreat. With the time that a retreat affords a team to pray and think and dream together, it's reasonable to consider allocating enough quality time for praying, dreaming, and writing out the proposed actions. Maximize the planning retreat by being fully prepared with an agenda that will achieve your desired results and watch what God does in your midst. And determine when, where, and how you will continue the process post-retreat.

Meetings

It can be painful to endure a poorly led meeting. Team meetings without life and energy are a drag that people dread attending. Meetings that have not been well planned or executed are close to intolerable. Add to that the inability to make decisions, the varying commitment levels of members to the team, the apparent lack of purpose for the meeting, and the difficult personalities around the table, and you're headed for disaster.

How can you ensure that team meetings have some sizzle or pizzazz or in some way draw members to attend? Here are a few suggestions to consider:

- *Timed agenda.* State the start and stop times (I recommend that you not go much beyond two and one-half hours), with specific times for each item to be discussed.
- *Spiritual formation.* Be sure to take time at the beginning of your meeting to pray, reflect on the Word of God, and share from your personal journey of faith. There is no better way to unite a team than through biblical reflection, prayer, and dialogue on matters of the heart and soul.

- *Team development.* Whenever possible, introduce a topic for discussion that generates interest among the members and will train them in a particular issue you are facing in your ministry (for example, trends affecting the age group you are serving or specific skill-development training). This can often be done through reviewing an article or book together.
- *Ministry stories.* By far the best way to stimulate interest in a team meeting is to interject stories of life transformation from or about individuals the team is serving in the ministry.
- *Action items.* As the team makes decisions, assign team members to take the lead in fulfilling particular action steps and then record the names in the form of meeting minutes for follow-up and future planning efforts. Remember that commonsense thinking and follow-through are the two most important skills for effectively fulfilling your ministry (see chapter 6).
- *Relationship building.* Either before, during, or after the stated meeting time, take opportunities to spend time together in informal settings, such as meals, games, movies, outdoor activities, or any of a number of fun team-building experiences. The quality of your relationships will have a direct, proportional impact on your shared ministry endeavors.

If you follow these general guidelines, it will enhance your team meeting experience and will certainly garner and retain the interest of the members. Be creative in designing your meetings, keeping in mind the team's concerns and needs. Involve others in the planning and execution of the meetings, which helps to ensure full participation. Whenever possible, take some time to assess the quality of your team meeting experience and be willing to follow the suggestions of others. If you keep your team meetings inviting and engaging, it will enhance the quality of your team's journey with God, your team relationships, and your service to others.

Assessments

In Patrick Lencioni's wonderful book *The Five Dysfunctions of a Team*, he provides an excellent assessment tool that helps teams evaluate their susceptibility to the five dysfunctions. Put into positive language, Lencioni states that members of cohesive teams behave as follows:

They trust one another.

They engage in unfiltered conflict around ideas.

They commit to decisions and plans of action.

They hold one another accountable for delivering against those plans.

They focus on the achievement of collective results.[3]

To guard against a dysfunctional approach to team building, Lencioni proposes that each team member complete a simple diagnostic. Then the team should review the results together, discussing discrepancies in the responses and identifying any clear implications for the team. I have found this simple tool to be tremendously helpful.

Lencioni's assessment tool consists of statements that describe teams and team members.[4] The person taking the diagnostic must decide how closely the statement describes his or her team. Here are some sample statements:

Team members are passionate and unguarded in their discussion of issues.

Team members know what their peers are working on and how they contribute to the collective good of the team.

Team members willingly make sacrifices (such as budget, turf, head count) in their departments or areas of expertise for the good of the team.

Team meetings are compelling not boring.

Team members leave meetings confident that their peers are completely committed to the decisions that were agreed on, even if there was initial disagreement.

During team meetings, the most important—and difficult—issues are put on the table to be resolved.

Team members are slow to seek credit for their own contributions but quick to point out those of others.

I strongly recommend that you read Lencioni's book and use his assessment tool with your team. Taking the time to assess your progress as a team toward health and vitality is an exercise that every team should do at least occasionally. Learning together about improvements that will increase your effectiveness is a sign that you are well on the road to healthy ministry together. Be sure to make evaluation an ongoing priority for all concerned.

Activities

In addition to a basic team health assessment like Lencioni's, there are other ways a team can explore the traits of a healthy ministry team in a noncompetitive fashion. First introduced by Anne Freeman, a colleague who specializes in developing cooperative games for teams, these activities can be useful in a teaching or training setting. Try them with your team and then share them with other colleagues committed to building healthy teams.

Building Trust

Materials needed: One blindfold per person (5–8 persons total).

Instructions: Put a blindfold on each participant. The facilitator whispers in each person's ear an assigned number between 1 and the total number of participants in this exercise. Ask the group to figure out a way to get themselves into numerical order without saying a word to one another. Watch how the group communicates inaudibly—and creatively!

Lesson learned: To build trust with other team members, we need to learn how to communicate effectively with one another.

Emphasizing Empowerment

Materials needed: Small scraps of paper, pens, and one large balloon per person participating in this exercise (any number of people willing to join in the fun are welcome).

Instructions: Invite each person to write on a small scrap of paper his or her name and one prayer request for fulfilling his or her God-given role on the ministry team in this next month/ season/year (choose one timetable). Each person should put his or her scrap of paper in a balloon, blow the balloon up, and tie it tightly. Ask the group to tap their balloons into the air, keeping them up for as long as possible. When a balloon falls to the floor, it should be left there. After all the balloons have fallen or within a short time, each person should pop one balloon, read the prayer request, and find the person who wrote it. Form a circle with the person you are going to pray for to your left. Hold hands in a circle and ask each person to pray for the request noted either silently or audibly.

Lesson learned: Each member of the team is valued, gifted, and called to serve on the team. Team members need to be empowered to utilize all that God has given them within the context of the ministry. We need to come alongside one another with our love, prayers, and encouragement.

Underscoring Assimilation

Materials needed: Up to five small Nerf balls per group.

Instructions: Ask for five, seven, or nine volunteers to gather in a circle. Give one person a Nerf ball to begin tossing to the people in the circle. Explain that the participants cannot pass the ball to the person directly to their right or left. Each person must receive the ball as it's tossed around the circle. Ask the group to develop a consistent pattern of tossing the ball, remembering who tosses the ball to them and to whom they toss the ball. After they've practiced their tossing pattern, add another ball to the circle to be tossed, using the same pattern. Continue to add balls to the circle until five Nerf balls are being used. It's fun to watch how well the group can handle multiple balls circulating within their tossing pattern!

Lesson learned: As a team assimilates individuals and responsibilities into the life of the ministry, it's vitally important that the team work well with one another. Otherwise, there may be chaos.

Teaching Management

Materials needed: One small Legos or other multi-piece construction toy kit per group participating in this activity.

Instructions: Pass out the construction kits. Invite the members of each team to sort the pieces, read the instructions, and work together in constructing the toy. Ask that each person have at least one part to add or one responsibility to contribute (for example, reading the instructions or passing out the parts).

Lesson learned: Each ministry team has "things" to manage together to accomplish shared goals. In all management tasks, there is room for each member of the team to participate—in this case, reading instructions, organizing the parts, sharing in the task, practicing patience, and celebrating accomplishment. The designated leader of the team encourages each member to join in the management of each level of completing the goal.

Catalyzing Servanthood

Materials needed: None.

Instructions: In groups of three to five, share with one another what most excites you about the ministry month/season/year ahead (choose one timetable from which to invite sharing). Ask each member to discuss how he or she hopes to maintain that focus on serving others in the days ahead. Be sure to focus on anticipating life transformation—that's what healthy teams are all about!

Lesson learned: Serving others is the focused intentionality of healthy teams. In this exercise, stress the ways in which your team will come alongside others in their spiritual, relational, and ministry development. Be sure to listen for how the joy of serving others will sustain your team in this next season of service. Praying for one another and each person's anticipated goals will bond you together in the love of Christ.

Definition—One Last Time!

We've spent a lot of time together in this text, exploring the traits of a vital ministry team. I hope that what you've discovered has been helpful in the development of your team. I trust you have received these words with an open heart to learn and grow and lead your team into the health of relationships, witness, and service that God has in mind for you. My prayer is that the definition of a team that we've explored together will become a benchmark for you to evaluate the effectiveness of your team. Just to remind you one last time, here again is the definition of a healthy ministry team:

> A Christian ministry team is a manageable group of diversely gifted people who hold one another accountable to serve joyfully together for the glory of God by:
>
> - sharing a common mission
> - embodying the loving message of Christ
> - accomplishing a meaningful ministry
> - anticipating transformative results

Our loving Father desires that we become the body of Christ, where each part supports the others in love. For that goal to be achieved we need to remember that a healthy team *trusts, empowers, assimilates, manages,* and *serves* in ways that glorify the Father, reflect the radiance of the Spirit, and embody the loving example of Jesus. May this be true in your team and may you model for others what it means to be a healthy ministry team. We're all in this together!

> Become a healthier team, a team of love.
> Healthy teams are patient and kind.
> They do not envy or boast,
> They are not proud or rude.
> They are not self-seeking or easily angered
> And do not keep a record of wrongs.
> They do not delight in evil,
> But they rejoice with the truth.
> Healthy teams:
> Protect,
> Trust,
> Hope,
> Persevere.
> Healthy teams are people who love!

May these truths guide your team toward the goal of making Jesus smile as you serve him together as one.

Stand firm. Let nothing move you. Always give yourselves fully to the work of the Lord, because you know that your labor in the Lord is not in vain.

1 Corinthians 15:58

Be on your guard; stand firm in the faith; be men of courage; be strong. Do everything in love.

1 Corinthians 16:13–14

The grace of the Lord Jesus be with you. My love to all of you in Christ Jesus. Amen.

1 Corinthians 16:23–24

Overview

Five Traits of Vital Leadership

T rust
E mpower
A ssimilate
M anage
S erve

A Christian ministry team is a manageable group of diversely gifted people who hold one another accountable to serve joyfully together for the glory of God by:

- sharing a common mission
- embodying the loving message of Christ
- accomplishing a meaningful ministry
- anticipating transformative results

Healthy Teams **TRUST**

Build Trust through Community
Build Trust through Celebration
Build Trust through Communication
Build Trust through Conflict

Healthy Teams **EMPOWER**

Empower through Gifts and Passions
Empower through Defined Responsibilities
Empower through Teachability and Resourcing
Empower through Delegation and Accountability

Healthy Teams **ASSIMILATE**

Assimilate through Cross-Pollination
Assimilate through Others-Orientation
Assimilate through Systemic Direction
Assimilate through Ministry Multiplication

Healthy Teams **MANAGE**

Manage through Strategic Plans
Manage through SMART Goals
Manage through Systematic Administration
Manage through Results Evaluation

Healthy Teams **SERVE**

Serve through Heartfelt Prayer
Serve through Discernment of Need
Serve through Fulfillment of Call
Serve through Transformation of Life

www.HealthyTeam.net

Afterword

God made us in his image and likeness. He is three: Father, Son, Holy Spirit. The triune nature of our Creator explains why we are individuals who function best in groups—efficient groups. Since we are created in the image of a three-person, single being, we are most comfortable and effective with a good team. No doubt, we are one within ourselves, but none of us can fulfill our calling alone. We can only achieve our maximum potential with others. The triune God made us this way—individuals so interconnected that we are one.

God places all of us in families, and those family relationships, if wisely developed, encourage, empower, protect, and direct all of us. We are more likely to fulfill God's plan for our lives when our family is healthy and functional. Sociologists agree that people have the greatest opportunity to become successful if raised by their own biological parents in a healthy family environment. I don't want to overstate the obvious, but this concept is vital to understanding the importance of healthy teams. Family units are so foundational to our identity that we share the same last name. Why? To demonstrate that even though we are separate individuals, we are, in fact, one.

When the Bible talks about the church, it uses three metaphors: the church is a family, a building, and a body. Families are individuals that converge into a single body. Buildings are made up of distinct materials fitted together to produce one form. Bodies have different parts and wildly different functions, but they are all integral to the whole.

Efficient teams are integral to our destiny. In order for us to fulfill God's calling in our lives, we have to be able to relate to and connect with others in a healthy way. As the senior pastor of New Life Church in Colorado Springs, Colorado, and the president of our National Association of Evangelicals (NAE), I see the inevitable truth that authentic ministry is a team effort. I see some fail and others succeed. The difference between the former and the latter is an ability to build empowering, wholesome, constructive relationships that advance God's call and purpose.

Remember this: *our relationships with God and others determine everything about us*. Relationships are everything. We are who we are and we will be who we will be as a result of the relationships in our lives.

Ministry is nothing but relationships. No, that's not well put. Let me try again. Relationships are ministry. No, that's not right either. Let me try again. In order to be godly, my relationship with God and my relationships with others are central to everything I accomplish. That's better. As a minister, I know that genuine ministry flows only out of my relationships, not out of programs or my own personal skills. I love to build teams to complete ministry projects, but I often reflect that the most valuable aspect of the process is the opportunity to bring a team together—to find people, combine them, and let them flourish in the combination of their gifts. Ministry happens along the avenue created by the formation of the team.

Moses needed Aaron. Without Aaron, Moses couldn't communicate clearly, and he was too harsh. Without Aaron, Moses couldn't accomplish God's call. Aaron needed Moses too. Without Moses, Aaron was a people-pleasing weakling. He was a communicator but not a leader. Without Moses, Aaron had an inadequate inner core. But when Moses and Aaron were together in a team, the two of them changed the world forever. So did David and Jonathan. So did Paul and Timothy. So did Jesus and the disciples.

Leaders have to work hard for teams to succeed. Each member is complex and unique. Blending is difficult but necessary. The key issues of team development have been engagingly addressed in this book—trust, empowerment, assimilation, management, and service to others. As you have learned, the team-building process has its ups and downs. From firsthand experience and from observation of others and the Scriptures, we can see that building teams requires strategy, affection, and mutual respect, as well as a common purpose. Most experiences in wise team building are empowering and exciting. Some experiences, though, will prove disappointing. But because we are made in God's image and likeness—that is, because we need community to reflect the triune fullness of God—the benefits of a team far outweigh the downside.

Steve is a good friend and a great model for all of us. In his wisdom, he has given us an extremely balanced approach to team building. The principles in this book are helpful to both corporate teams and ministry teams—teams that result in intimacy with God and authenticity in the body of Christ.

Ted Haggard
Senior Pastor, New Life Church
President, National Association of Evangelicals
Colorado Springs, Colorado

Notes

Introduction The Truth about Teams

1. Peter Marshall, *Mr. Jones, Meet the Master* (New York: Revell, 1949), 57–58.

Chapter 1 The Bible and Teams

1. George Barna, *The Power of Team Leadership* (Colorado Springs: WaterBrook, 2001), 31.

Chapter 2 Overview of Healthy Teams

1. Dave Travis, "The Church Champions Update for July 21, 2000" (Dallas: Leadership Network). Used by permission.
2. Jon R. Katzenbach and Douglas K. Smith, *The Wisdom of Teams* (New York: Harper Business, 1994), 214.
3. George Cladis, *Leading the Team-Based Church* (San Francisco: Jossey-Bass, 1999), 16.
4. Katzenbach and Smith, *The Wisdom of Teams*, 91–92.
5. Adapted from an article by Gary McIntosh, "Effective Teams in the Twenty-first Century," at www.Christianity.com (Dec. 20, 2000).

Chapter 3 Healthy Teams Trust

1. Patrick Lencioni, *The Five Dysfunctions of a Team* (San Francisco: Jossey-Bass, 2002), 197.
2. For more information on this topic, please see my book *Becoming a Healthy Disciple: Ten Traits of a Vital Christian* (Grand Rapids: Baker, 2004).
3. Donald W. Morgan, *Share the Dream, Build the Team* (Grand Rapids: Baker, 2001), 149–50.
4. John C. Maxwell, *The Seventeen Indisputable Laws of Teamwork* (Nashville: Thomas Nelson, 2001), 202.
5. Ibid, 203–4.

6. John Trent, with Rodney Cox and Eric Tooker, *Leading from Your Strengths: Building Close-Knit Ministry Teams* (Nashville: Broadman and Holman, 2004), 84.

7. Lencioni, *Five Dysfunctions of a Team*, 202–3.

8. Ibid., 204.

Chapter 4 Healthy Teams Empower

1. William Barclay, *The Letters to the Corinthians*, Daily Study Bible Series (Philadelphia: Westminster, 1975), 14–15.

2. Wayne Cordeiro, *Doing Church as a Team* (Ventura, CA: Regal, 2001), 67.

3. Ibid., 67–72.

4. Ibid., 32–33.

5. "Billy Graham's Soulmate: Life Together," *Christianity Today* (July 9, 2001), 26–27.

6. Lencioni, *Five Dysfunctions of a Team*, 214.

Chapter 5 Healthy Teams Assimilate

1. Emmanuel Gospel Center mission statement at www.egc.org/about/.

2. Ibid.

3. Barclay, *Letters to the Corinthians*, 113–14.

4. Ibid., 114–15.

5. Lencioni, *Five Dysfunctions of a Team*, 52–53.

6. *Bits and Pieces* (Sept. 19, 1991), 5–6 at http://www.bible.org/illus.asp?topic_id=1529.

7. Peter Senge, *The Fifth Discipline* (New York: Doubleday, 1990); Peter Senge, *The Fifth Discipline Fieldbook* (New York: Doubleday, 1994).

Chapter 6 Healthy Teams Manage

1. R. Alec Mackenzie, *Teamwork through Time Management* (Chicago: Dartnell Corporation, 1990), 153.

2. Keith Beasley-Topliffe, ed., *The Upper Room Dictionary of Christian Spiritual Formation* (Nashville: Upper Room, 2003), 81.

3. Ibid., 82.

4. Cordeiro, *Doing Church as a Team*, 120.

5. Ibid., 136–37.

6. More details on the strategic planning process can be gleaned from a thorough review of Stephen A. Macchia, *Becoming a Healthy Church Workbook* (Grand Rapids: Baker, 2001).

7. Lencioni, *Five Dysfunctions of a Team*, 218–19.

Chapter 7 Healthy Teams Serve

1. John Piper, *The Dangerous Duty of Delight* (Sisters, OR: Multnomah, 2001), 44–45.

2. Ibid., 79–80.

3. Dietrich Bonhoeffer, *Life Together* (San Francisco: Harper and Row, 1954), 37.

4. Ibid., based on chapter 4, "Ministry," 90–109.

5. Rueben P. Job, *A Guide to Spiritual Discernment* (Nashville: Upper Room Books, 1996), 36–37.

Chapter 8 Leading Healthy Teams

1. Michael Youseff, *The Leadership Style of Jesus* (Colorado Springs: Victor, 1986), 35–36 (emphasis mine).

2. Cordeiro, *Doing Church as a Team,* 112.

3. Charles M. Olsen and Ellen Morseth, *Selecting Church Leaders* (Nashville: Upper Room Books, 2002), 72–73.

4. Maxwell, *Seventeen Indisputable Laws of Teamwork,* 218–19.

5. George Barna, *The Power of Team Leadership*, 138–41.

6. Katzenbach and Smith, *The Wisdom of Teams,* 138–44.

7. This definition of a team leader is adapted from the chapter "Servant Leadership Development" in Stephen A. Macchia, *Becoming a Healthy Church* (Grand Rapids: Baker, 1999).

8. Adapted from Henri J. M. Nouwen, *In the Name of Jesus* (New York: Crossroad, 1998), 71–73.

Conclusion Becoming a Healthier Team

1. Cladis, *Leading the Team-Based Church,* 160–61.

2. Maxwell, *Seventeen Indisputable Laws of Teamwork,* 185.

3. Lencioni, *Five Dysfunctions of a Team,* 189–90.

4. Ibid., 192–94.

Selected Bibliography

Barna, George. *The Power of Team Leadership*. Colorado Springs: WaterBrook Press, 2001.

Cladis, George. *Leading the Team-Based Church*. San Francisco: Jossey-Bass, 1999.

Cordeiro, Wayne. *Doing Church as a Team*. Ventura, CA: Regal, 2001.

Katzenbach, Jon R., and Douglas K. Smith. *The Wisdom of Teams*. New York: Harper Collins, 1994.

Lencioni, Patrick. *The Five Dysfunctions of a Team*. San Francisco: Jossey-Bass, 2002.

Macchia, Stephen A. *Becoming a Healthy Church*. Grand Rapids: Baker, 1999.

Macchia, Stephen A. *Becoming a Healthy Church Workbook*. Grand Rapids: Baker, 2001.

Mackenzie, R. Alec. *Teamwork through Time Management*. Chicago: Dartnell Corporation, 1990.

MacMillan, Pat. *The Performance Factor*. Nashville: Broadman and Holman, 2001.

Maxwell, John C. *The Seventeen Indisputable Laws of Teamwork*. Nashville: Thomas Nelson, 2001.

Morgan, Donald W. *Share the Dream, Build the Team: Ten Keys to Revitalizing Your Church*. Grand Rapids: Baker, 2001.

Trent, John, with Rodney Cox and Eric Tooker. *Leading from Your Strengths: Building Close-Knit Ministry Teams*. Nashville: Broadman and Holman, 2004.

The Rev. Dr. **Stephen A. Macchia** is founding president of Leadership Transformations, Inc. He also serves as the director of the Pierce Center for Disciple-Building and teaches in the Doctor of Ministry program at Gordon-Conwell Theological Seminary. In these capacities he comes alongside pastors, leaders, and ministry teams in their spiritual formation and ministry discernment needs. He serves on a number of national ministry boards and is a spiritual director, seminar leader, retreat facilitator, church consultant, and leadership coach.

Dr. Macchia is the fortunate husband of Ruth and the proud father of two children, Nathan and Rebekah.

For more information on Dr. Macchia's ministry, please visit: www.LeadershipTransformations.org or www.HealthyTeam .net.

Other books by Stephen A. Macchia

Becoming a Healthy Church
Becoming a Healthy Church Workbook
Becoming a Healthy Church Leaders Kit
Becoming a Healthy Disciple
Becoming a Healthy Disciple Small Group
 Study and Worship Guide

Also Available from

STEPHEN A. MACCHIA

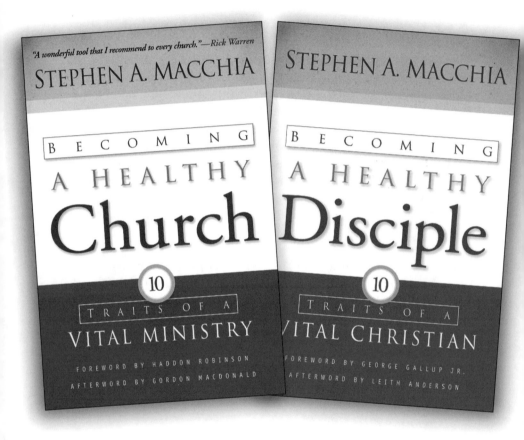

M ake a positive change in your life and the life of your church. With these great resources from spiritual formation expert Stephen Macchia, you and your church can be on the road to true health, growth, and discipleship.

BakerBooks
www.bakerbooks.com
Available at your local bookstore.